D0239540

THE COMPLETE GUIDE TO BUSINESS AND STRATEGIC PLANNING

For Voluntary Organisations

By Alan Lawrie

A Directory of Social Change production

THE COMPLETE GUIDE TO BUSINESS
AND STRATEGIC PLANNING

For Voluntary Organisations

By Alan Lawrie

Published by the Directory of Social Change, Radius Works, Back Lane, London NW3 1HL.

Published 1994.

Copyright © 1994 The Directory of Social Change.

No part of this book may be stored in a retrieval system or reproduced in any form whatsoever without prior permission in writing from the publisher. The Directory of Social Change is registered charity no 800517.

ISBN 1 873860 61 7

BRITISH LIBRARY CATALOGUING IN PUBLICATION DATA
A catalogue record for this book is available from the British Library.

Designed and typeset by Kate Bass.

Printed and bound by Page Bros., Norfolk.

Supported by

♻ National Westminster Bank
We're here to make life easier

People join, work and contribute to charities and other voluntary organisations for a variety of reasons, perhaps seldom considering that only through efficient and effective management can the ultimate aims of those organisations be achieved.

Without clear objectives and careful planning, organisations can fail their donors and clients. Careful attention to the elements of any successful enterprise, such as proper planning, resource allocation, and management ensures that charities and voluntary organisations realise their potential. Otherwise, valuable time and effort can be lost - and the only people who pay for ineffective management of a voluntary organisation are the people or causes it sets out to assist in the first place.

NatWest has long recognised the vital importance of the contributions made by charities and voluntary organisations to society, through our community investment programme. Through this and our extensive banking relationships with charities, we recognise the pressures that charities and voluntary organisations are under to meet increasing demands for their services. We want to make our contribution to helping the voluntary sector to meet this challenge. Natwest's own experience has led us to the view that a critical success factor in any venture is access to sound practical advice; that is why we are pleased to support this publication. Good luck with your business planning.

MARTIN GRAY
CHIEF EXECUTIVE, UK BRANCH BUSINESS

National Westminster Bank

FOREWORD

The need for this book is reflected in the changing circumstances of many voluntary organisations. The ever-increasing need to obtain funding, to negotiate contracts and to convince people that their organisation is worth investing in requires new skills and new processes. Simply borrowing techniques from other sectors will not work well enough for you.

The planning process involves many different issues. Balancing competing needs and coping with many different expectations are very much at the heart of managing organisations which do not have a profit motive. This book does not offer an off the shelf blueprint for drawing up a strategic or business plan. Instead it provides you with the tools, frameworks and techniques that you can easily apply to your organisation to develop and draw up your own plan.

Much of the book is based on practical experience of different agencies that I have worked with as a consultant and trainer. I am grateful to many friends and clients who allowed me time to talk over their experience. I would also like to thank the Directory of Social Change for stimulating this project and particularly thank Jan Mellor for her advice and support throughout.

Alan Lawrie is an independent consultant and trainer who works with public sector and voluntary agencies on management, organisational and strategic development.

CONTENTS

INTRODUCTION

WHAT THIS BOOK IS ABOUT

This book is about three things.

❶ It aims to help voluntary organisations make clear decisions about their future direction and priorities.

❷ It introduces some tools for strategic planning and management.

❸ It explains how to draw up and use a business plan.

WHY THINK ABOUT BUSINESS PLANS?

There are several entry points to the book's subject:

❶ The tougher funding climate and the growth of a "contract culture" have led some funders to require the production of a "business plan" before they consider a funding application.

Business plans have their roots in the private sector and are an essential requirement in persuading lenders to back an enterprise. In recent years, like many other management concepts, they have crossed from the profit making sector to the "not for profit" sector.

❷ A recognition by many voluntary organisations that the constant rate of change and consequent uncertainty means that the organisation cannot stand still.

Many managers and increasingly some trustees are expressing the need to clarify what their organisation is about, decide what is and is not a priority for the limited resources that exist and set out a direction for the organisation's future. This kind of management is different from dealing with the day to day demands of making sure that the organisation keeps operating. Strategic management is hard. It requires clear thinking, clarity of purpose and to win the commitment of others and convince them that it is not some academic or "pie in the sky" exercise.

❸ The arrival at a point where decisions have to be made about the organisation's future.

A director of one charity described her role as like "riding a roller coaster that never arrives anywhere, but, only gets faster". Changes in legislation, new funding, short term priorities and new ways of working mean that organisations can easily become reactive to external events and be pulled into activities that either do not fit with the rest of the organisation or are a departure from their original aims. Those charged with the management and direction of the organisation need to take a grip on what they are doing. They need to decide where they are going and not simply respond to external events.

All organisations are going somewhere. The future direction could be about the organisation getting bigger or smaller, working in a particular way or doing more or less of a particular activity. The main theme behind this book is that the people who are charged with managing a voluntary organisation need to ensure that they set the direction and agree strategies for where they want to be.

WHY DO IT?

There are many reasons not to draw up a business plan or think strategically.

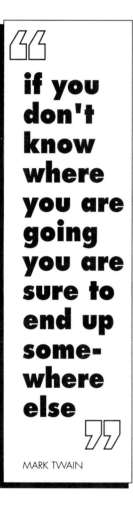

> if you don't know where you are going you are sure to end up some-where else
>
> MARK TWAIN

◆ Just keeping operating on a day to day basis is often enough of a struggle.

◆ The language of organisational planning is often off putting.

◆ The word "business" might be objectionable to some people.

◆ The difficulty of planning in a period of constant change

◆ The fear of finding that the "goal posts keep moving"

◆ The lack of skills or resources to implement the plan.

The following six points explain the thinking behind this book and might suggest reasons why voluntary agencies should spend valuable time on this process.

A PARADOX ABOUT PLANNING

There is a paradox about planning. The harder it is to plan the more important clear planning becomes. Uncertainty about funding, lack of clear direction, a reliance on what was done in the past as the basis for deciding what to do next and a vision that stops at the end of the current financial year mean that an organisation can easily become motionless. It spends its time hoping that things will get better. In effect, it becomes governed by what it did in the past rather than what it wants to do in the future. It becomes predictable and paralysed in a rapidly changing world. At some stage someone needs to be bold enough to suggest a direction to go in and agree a plan for achieving it.

DIRECTION PLANNING RATHER THAN A DETAILED BLUEPRINT

In the 1960s and 1970s large corporations and public agencies invested heavily in corporate planning. These planners produced comprehensive ten-year documents that even in more stable times became quickly out of date or even were out of date the day that they left the printers. Our capacity to predict the future accurately is very limited. This book is concerned with helping organisations clarify their long and short term goals, explore possible future possibilities and make a case why others should have confidence in their organisation. It is the process that is important rather than the product.

THE PROCESS AND THE RESULTS MATTER RATHER THAN WHAT IT IS CALLED

The idea to produce a business plan sometimes causes cynicism amongst a staff team. Is it just another imported management fad that someone has picked up on a course? How the process is managed and how people are involved in it has a considerable bearing on the result. Later in this book the difference between first order change and second order change is explored. First order change is when an organisation or individual appears to be doing something differently. Second order change is when we start behaving differently and genuinely commit ourselves to the process of change. Many business plans get stuck at first order change. A plan is produced by a few people, it is published, briefly discussed, filed away and quickly forgotten about. This book is concerned not only with producing a credible plan, but also with ensuring that the plan feels real and relevant to people in to the organisation. Whether it is called a business plan, a strategic plan or a forward plan is not important.

THE DANGERS OF SHORT-TERMISM

Political changes, annual budgets and short-term funding can make any notion of planning difficult. Part of thinking strategically is to keep in touch with day to day realities and opportunities, but at the same time to focus on future needs and directions. The one thing that is certain is that everything will remain uncertain. Secure and committed long term funding is doubtful and difficult to achieve. Political and economic stability is unlikely with constant re-organisations, friction between central and local government and a chronic shortage of funds. The profile and expectations of an organisation's users are unlikely to become fixed. There is a real danger of voluntary organisations losing a longer-term perspective, becoming driven by short-term demands and only dealing with what is urgent rather than what is important. Just having a short-term perspective could make a voluntary organisation's existence vulnerable.

During research for this book, a local authority officer with responsibility for grant aiding local voluntary groups said that "Most of the organisations I deal with would be very easy to cut, and if cut, could close quickly. They are geared up from April to April. They are fearful of taking on longer-term commitments. They employ their staff on short-term contracts (that in practice are often renewed). They have no contingencies. They operate almost as if they expect to be closed down at a moments notice."

More and more managing is about accepting uncertainty as a norm, but, having the confidence to chart a longer term direction.

GOOD PLANNING BUILDS ON WHAT YOU DO ALREADY

All too often, plans degenerate into a "wish list" of how we would like things to be in a perfect world. The frameworks and ideas suggested in this book aim to make sure that any plan takes into account the realities of the organisation in its present situation. You need to ensure that the plan is realistic and sets out clear steps for its implementation. Too often business plans only consist of catchy mission statements without any real evidence that the organisation has worked out how to move forward.

MAKING THE CASE FOR THE ORGANISATION

Often a voluntary agency suffers from a credibility gap. The outside world sees it as being made up of well intentioned amateurs. Funders insist on rigorous and bureaucratic controls on how "their" money is being spent. Sometimes this rubs off on the staff and volunteers who fail to see fully the effectiveness and efficiency of their efforts or that they are achieving incredible results with minimal resources. A central part of a business plan is to make the case for the organisation. It sets out the track record of the organisation, demonstrates that it has effective systems, people and processes in place and that it can deliver results. Voluntary organisations are increasingly being called upon to show (often through producing a business plan), that they will be a reliable partner in a contract or funding agreement. The process of drawing up a business plan often helps an organisation to value itself more and be more "assertive" with the outside world.

THE PLANNING PROCESS IN OUTLINE

Stage ❶ : Clarification of the purpose and mission of the organisation, is about ensuring that there is a clear sense of direction and agreement about the core values that unite an organisation. The decisions reached in this stage should act as an anchor for the rest of the process. **Chapter three** suggests how an organisation can renew its overall purpose, considers the dangers of simply being driven by what was done in the past and gives some practical hints on drawing up a mission statement.

Stage ❷ : The information gathering process is an attempt to take stock of the organisation to date. **Chapter four** looks at ways of collecting information about the organisation's current activities, its financial and its management performance, and also suggests ways of predicting how services might develop. It looks at the external environment, and considers how future trends and events might impact on an organisation's future. **Chapter five** reviews the financial information that is needed to accurately plan. It looks at ways of costing work, managing cash flow and the strategic management of finance.

Stage ❸ : Considers how to use this information to identify key assumptions, strategic choices and direction. This stage, discussed in **Chapter six,** is a critical one. Informed by a review of internal and external trends, key people in the organisation need to identify choices open to them, evaluate them and agree a direction. This is often a painful process as it usually involves saying

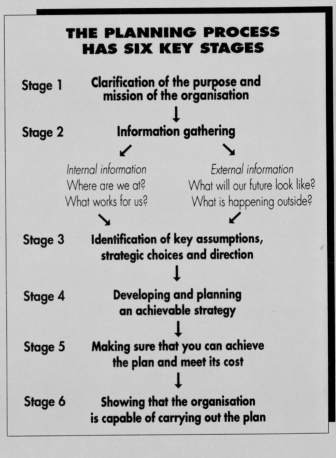

THE PLANNING PROCESS HAS SIX KEY STAGES

Stage 1   Clarification of the purpose and mission of the organisation

↓

Stage 2   Information gathering

↙   ↘

Internal information
Where are we at?
What works for us?

External information
What will our future look like?
What is happening outside?

↘   ↙

Stage 3   Identification of key assumptions, strategic choices and direction

↓

Stage 4   Developing and planning an achievable strategy

↓

Stage 5   Making sure that you can achieve the plan and meet its cost

↓

Stage 6   Showing that the organisation is capable of carrying out the plan

what an organisation will stop doing or will not get involved in.

Stage 4 : Developing and planning an achievable strategy is about making realistic choices about the future and creating a coherent plan. **Chapter six** suggests several processes for developing strategy.

Stage 5 : Making sure that you can achieve the plan and meet its costs is about the feasibility of planning. **Chapter six** also looks at how to work from the priorities agreed in the previous stage, draw up clear objectives for each one and identify the organisational and management processes needed to meet the plan.

Stage 6 : Showing that the organisation is capable of carrying out the plan, requires the organisation to show that it has in place the structures, systems and skills needed to implement the plan. **Chapter seven** suggests various sources of evidence that an organisation can use in its plan and shows how this information can be used to persuade funders and others to back the organisation.

Chapter eight gives guidance on writing a plan and provides a template and content list for a plan.

Chapter nine demonstrates the importance of making sure that the plan is implemented, looks at how it can be used to steer and change the organisation and suggests how managers can use, monitor and update the plan.

Sources of further help, a resource guide and a reading list are provided at the end of the book.

STARTING THE PROCESS

The process by which the plan is developed and prepared has a critical impact on its successful implementation. Practical experience consistently shows that the sooner that people potentially affected by change are involved in the process the more likely it is that change will be implemented and followed through.

In planning, there is a tendency for a few select individuals to isolate themselves from others, produce a detailed plan written in an inaccessible "management speak" and then become frustrated when no-one takes the plan seriously.

As Bertolt Brecht wrote, "The finest plans are often spoilt by the pettiness of those who are supposed to carry them out, since even emperors can do nothing without the support of their soldiers".

However, it often seems as if the more people that are involved, the harder it is to manage the process. Meetings become longer, difficult decisions are avoided, the process gets delayed, and innovation is strangled by so called consultation and consensus.

One way to resolve this problem is to think of the process as having three levels.

❶ A downward direction setting out boundaries and criteria for the plan.

Trustees and managers need to agree the mission and core values. They need to set a broad organisational context for the plan. This level is about steering a direction for the rest of the plan.

❷ Direct input from front line workers & volunteers.

People working in the organisation should be able to contribute and participate in the "big picture" discussions about mission and values. Once these have been set they should then be able to develop specific plans for their unit or department in the light of the overall direction.

❸ Lateral team working both inside and outside the organisation.

Groups of staff, users and committee members can work together to carry out specific aspects of the process such as identifying future trends or exploring possible future scenarios for the organisation.

The whole process of involvement, consultation and participation needs to be tightly managed. If not, the process will quickly degenerate into endless meetings and many bold ideas will be killed by unmanaged consultation.

Careful timetabling, effective delegation of responsibilities and external help with the process may well be needed.

Managers need to take the responsibility for setting out the direction for the organisation, agreeing key priorities and ensuring that the plan is produced to time and in a cohesive format.

The detailed implementation of the strategy, the production of specific or tactical plans, or the feasibility studies of a project are often best delegated to the people who will have to work on them (and therefore know most about them).

Managers need to ensure that what they produce is in line with the overall strategy of the plan, is realistic, challenging and achievable.

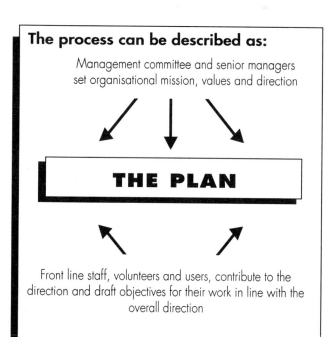

The process can be described as:

Management committee and senior managers set organisational mission, values and direction

THE PLAN

Front line staff, volunteers and users, contribute to the direction and draft objectives for their work in line with the overall direction

It might also be feasible to involve people who do not directly work in the organisation. Users, carers, supporters and even funders might bring a valuable insight and stop an organisation becoming complacent or inward looking. External consultants can also be engaged to help with the process.

A housing project had two different experiences of producing a business plan. Its first attempt, motivated simply because the Housing Corporation requested it, was the product of hard labour by the director and the finance manager working together. Few people ever referred to the plan or felt that they had any connection to it.

The next attempt was different. A joint team made up of two committee members, the director, the finance manager and one person from each of the project's three teams produced a mission statement and carried out a review of internal and external developments. The next management committee agreed a brief paper from the director setting out likely assumptions and suggesting five core priorities. For the next six weeks the three work teams had to draw up and cost detailed and measurable plans for their team's work. The director's role was to act as a coach for them in this process, sometimes pushing them further, but often making sure that they were being realistic. The final plan was produced by a small team led by the finance manager.

The project's director commented that his role had "been more about thinking about the big picture than about the detail. I had to "hold the ring" on the process and make sure that the plan was an integral product produced on time. It was very difficult for me to stand back and not take the plan over. Two early benefits have been that people now do refer to how their work fits into the plan; and each team now has a work plan which they monitor, but, feel a commitment to as they were the main force in setting it".

AGREEING OBJECTIVES FOR THE PLAN

Often there is a lack of confidence or cynicism about the planning process. Most of us have had enough experience of plans that create paper and lead to no action. One starting point is to agree some objectives for the business planning process itself. The task of agreeing these objectives might help to clarify the internal and external reasons why a plan is needed and create an opportunity to measure its value in time.

Although it is probably much better to work out your own, possible objectives for business planning might include:

◆ To clarify long term aims.

◆ To relate all activities to aims.

◆ To develop a realistic future strategy.

◆ To make measurable plans.

◆ To link future developments in the external environment to internal change.

◆ To convince financial backers that the organisation is credible.

All organisations are changing all the time

This chart shows the "emergent strategies" of a youth agency (i.e. how things change over time.)

TREND	PROBABLE REASON	STRATEGIC QUESTION
Less outreach work. Now only working with those who come to us.	Pressure of keeping the centre open for ten sessions - funder says that is what is important.	What should be the balance between the centre and field work?
More in depth work with fewer young people.	Two workers have trained in counselling and want to practice it.	Is this what we are supposed to be doing?
More young black women using centre.	Possibly because we employed a woman worker who is black.	What would happen if she left?
More work with 13 - 16 age group.	Because older age group are into other things.	Who should be our target groups?
More time on fund raising.	Funders will not pay core costs.	Should we find better ways of making our case?
Doing more work on drug misuse.	Because there are funds available for this work	How could this develop? Do we want to do more or less of this?

A starting point for the process itself is to deal with the often held belief that strategic planning is impossible. The management writer Henry Mintzberg, talks about how all organisations are moving in some direction even if they do not know it or have not planned it. This is sometimes called an emergent strategy.

A useful exercise is to ask participants to think back over the past few years and to try to identify what sort of directions the organisation has moved in and is currently moving in. Discussion should focus on what has driven the organisation, what has controlled it and what choices have been subconsciously made by individuals and teams.

The exercise can help to illustrate the point that although we can not always control the detail, the organisation is moving and it is better to chart its path than let it happen by accident.

THE LANGUAGE OF BUSINESS PLANNING

Different writers use words like goals, aims and objectives differently. There is no standard textbook definition. The important thing is to ensure that the terms that are used are defined and understood and that they are used consistently.

This book uses four main terms to describe the planning process.

❶ The Mission: This is a brief statement of overall purpose and values. It is the reason why the organisation continues to exist. It says little about what, how, or when an organisation will do something. Mission statements should be a long term statement of intent that follow on from the original vision that inspired the organisation.

❷ Strategic Aims: These set out the direction for the organisation. They are a statement of the key priorities for the organisation in the immediate to medium-term future. Everything the organisation does should be related back to a strategic aim.

❸ **The Operational Objectives:** These are detailed, costed and timed plans of what the organisation will do under each strategic aim. They set out a work plan for the organisation.

❹ **Critical Success Factors:** These are the things that the organisation has to get right in order to achieve its aims and objectives. They usually relate to internal processes, systems and people factors.

These are all described in greater detail in later chapters.

HOW LONG TO PLAN FOR?

The question of how long to plan for is a difficult, but obvious question. Most business plans produced these days are usually written for anywhere between one year and five years ahead. Various factors will influence how long to plan for. For example it is reasonable to expect a housing association which may be involved in several capital building or development projects to plan for a longer period of time than a campaigning organisation dealing with changing politics, volatile public opinion and legislative timetables.

One approach is to adopt a plan that rolls forward. An organisation might decide that it can be confident that it's mission will still be relevant in three to five years time. It can also probably also identify some strategic aims that will take it nearer to its mission that will also last for two to three years. However, it might decide to produce an annual plan listing specific objectives for the next twelve months that will become its action plan.

THE LANGUAGE OF PLANNING

The terms used in this book need some explanation. You might find it useful to note down what each term currently means to you. What is your organisation's vision, mission, strategy and direction? and who is responsible for them.

VISION

The reason why the organisation was established and why it continues to exist. What does it want to change or protect? What makes it distinctive from other organisations?

MISSION

The organisation's current sense of purpose and goal. It should also include a statement of organisational values - the beliefs and ethics that hold it together. The mission should be the driving force behind all the activities.

STRATEGY

The sense of priorities and direction for the organisation over the next period. A series of connected aims that set out an immediate direction for all aspects of the organisation.

OBJECTIVES

The detailed work plan and action plans that will enable the organisation to implement its strategy. They should be clear and measurable and indicate when and how the objective will be carried out.

WHY DO IT?

What are your motives for spending time on producing a plan?

What do you want the plan to achieve?

Are your motives mainly internally driven ("we want to decide where we are going") **or are they imposed on you by external forces** (eg. a funder demands a business plan)**?**

What will be your criteria for judging the success of the plan itself and the planning process?

WHAT ARE WE ABOUT?

Almost all voluntary organisations will have a written constitution which says something about their aims, purpose or goals. What is written in the constitution is legally what the organisation is for. This seems a logical starting point for any planning exercise. However, sometimes this is insufficient. Constitutional aims and objectives are often written in a legal or archaic language which may not be comprehensible. Some constitutions are drafted to allow a broad range of possible activities within a legal structure. Some were written so long ago that they do not "feel" like they have anything to do with the organisation.

In the past ten years mission statements have become increasingly popular as a management tools. Perhaps it all started with probably the best known mission statement, that of The USS Enterprise's on television's Star Trek "To boldly go......".

Many organisations have invested time in producing catchy expressions of their purpose. Often the process generates a degree of cynicism. The statement is often little more than a vague slogan, or it has all the certainty of a New Year resolution.

Sometimes the term "mission" is met with scepticism. It is seen as being a trendy idea and a quick fix technique. Management trends and fads never seem to stop. Some management "experts" now talk of "mission drift", when an organisation has stopped following its original mission and started dabbling in other activities and sidelines.

There is a strong argument for ensuring that all the people in an organisation have the same sense of purpose and vision. Work spent on defining the mission can have the following benefits:

◆ It sets out a longer-term perspective.

◆ It can create unity around a common vision and identity.

◆ It makes it clear for insiders and outsiders what the organisation is about and what it isn't about.

◆ It creates an overall sense of purpose from which strategy and action can follow.

Discussion of mission and vision can cause tension and conflict. Some voluntary organisations have become very good at pretending to be all things to all people.

It is not unusual to find different people in the organisation having very different ideas about what is important and what the organisation's priorities should be. Does a community advice centre exist to inform people of their rights? Or to encourage self help? Or to campaign for social change? Or to counsel people with problems? It may well be possible to do all of these things successfully for a period of time. But, when it comes to making decisions about future priorities, future targets or future direction, it is important to have a common view of the organisation's purpose and priorities. If the organisation pretends to do everything, it could well end up fragmented and overstretched.

Three activities are useful for discussing and arriving at a common view:

❶ Identifying what drives the organisation.

❷ Identifying what is (or should) be unique about the organisation.

❸ Describing the organisation's work in terms of outcomes rather than activities.

A MISGUIDED MISSION

The director of a regional museum did not expect much discussion when he tabled his draft "mission statement" at the quarterly trustees meeting. The trustees were mainly academics or amateur historians who had little time for management ideas.

The draft described the mission as :

"To be a lively, open and popular educational experience. To display our collection in a creative and exciting way. To ensure that the museum is open and accessible to local people."

The chair of the trustees expressed concern that there was no mention of scholarly pursuits or of preserving the museum's collection for common heritage. One trustee said that the mission statement would be more suited to a theme park rather than a centre for study and historical research.

The director thought back over previous trustees meetings. There had been some criticism of his proposal to recruit a marketing officer rather than fill a vacant curator's post. Another disagreement was over spending money on a schools education pack rather than on extending the collection. The trustees showed no interest in his performance measures which showed a steady rise in visitors, they only seemed concerned with the academic credentials of the staff and the quality of the collection.

At the end of the meeting the director agreed to redraft the mission statement in the light of the discussion. No doubt, he would be able to come up with a compromise set of words that would meet his desire to have a lively and popular museum and the trustees concern for academic excellence.

Three questions worried him.

❶ Would the compromise wording work in practice or was he just avoiding a fundamental difference which should be resolved in a more substantial way?

❷ Was it possible to "direct" an organisation where people were being asked to face in different directions?

❸ Could the two approaches be brought together or would the conflict boil away?

WHAT DRIVES THE ORGANISATION?

Voluntary organisations are driven by other things than simply making money. With many voluntary organisations run largely

AVOIDING A GOAL

Writing in the January - February 1987 edition of the Harvard Business Review, Philip D Harvey and James D Snyder stress the importance of charities having a clear goal for their organisations. They identify six reasons why for some "not for profit" agencies clear goal definition is often elusive:

① The fear of accountability. Having a clear goal increases the visibility of managers. They become more accountable.

② Many organisations continue to have projects when they no longer serve the goal. Winding an activity up can be very painful, so something which accomplishes little is allowed to continue.

③ Taking on an activity because money is available. The availability of funding becomes the driving force, not goals or needs.

④ A fear that management science may replace romance: "Won't hard nosed evaluation undermine humanitarian instincts?"

⑤ A lot of time in voluntary agencies is spent on tasks which do not fit into any identifiable goal. Servicing meetings, encouraging goodwill, liaison with other bodies, public relations and meeting requests for information all make it easy for the organisation to be distracted from its mission.

⑥ That the financial indicators that a profit making company has are less meaningful in a voluntary agency. They say little about progress towards the goal.

reproduced with the permission of the Harvard Business Review

or even entirely by paid staff, the term "voluntary" may come to feel less and less relevant. The term "not for profit" is often used instead. It seems odd to describe an organisation by what it does not aim to do rather than what it is for!

In an organisation there are usually lots of different things driving it at the same time. One way of looking at it is to identify three possible driving forces:

① **Values driven.**

② **Resource driven.**

③ **Innovation driven.**

① VALUES DRIVEN

The values driven element is the sense of commitment and shared understanding that holds the organisation together. Values are important in creating a sense of common vision and purpose. However, too much attention to values could lead to the organisation becoming so "pure" and inward looking that very little ever gets done. Values on their own do not pay peoples wages.

② RESOURCE DRIVEN

The resource element is the capacity of the organisation to fund and staff its activities. Sometimes this is a drive to get bigger and expand by attracting more and more resources, although there is now a growing recognition that just because an organisation is getting bigger it does not mean that it is any more effective.

③ INNOVATION DRIVEN

The innovation element is the organisation's capacity to innovate, take risks and be creative. Many voluntary organisations came into existence to do things that a public sector agency or private company would regard as not sensible practice or too dangerous to invest funds in. Over time, organisations often become safer places and start to reject ideas and innovations that could challenge the status quo. Innovative organisations can be exciting, dynamic and fun. They can also be chaotic, crisis driven and place considerable stress on individuals.

Some questions that emerge from this exercise:

- ◆ What currently drives your organisation?

- ◆ Which of these factors do you think is most important?

- ◆ How do you manage to combine all the three elements together?

- ◆ Which of these are going to be important for the organisation's future?

WHAT IS UNIQUE ABOUT THE ORGANISATION?

In a commercial organisation a common marketing technique is to identify a product's USP. Its unique selling proposition. In simple commercial terms it is what makes one washing powder different from another. The difference can be a tangible one (it performs better) or a matter of perception ("it feels right for me").

It is an interesting exercise to pose the question "what is unique about our service" and to try to list the factors that make the organisation distinctive. What would happen if the services were discontinued or the organisation ceased to exist? Would any alternatives be available? Would clients be better or worse off? Would the organisation have to be reinvented?

Some business organisations have formed their mission statement around the characteristics and factors that makes them distinct from other competitors in their market. Work on its "uniqueness" often helps an organisation to develop a strong sense of identity that holds it together internally and clarifies its purpose externally.

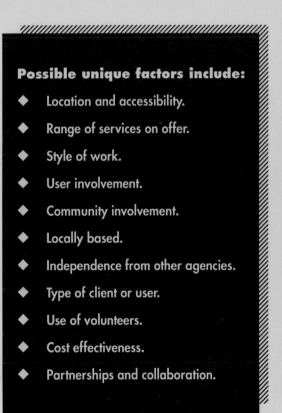

Possible unique factors include:

- ◆ Location and accessibility.

- ◆ Range of services on offer.

- ◆ Style of work.

- ◆ User involvement.

- ◆ Community involvement.

- ◆ Locally based.

- ◆ Independence from other agencies.

- ◆ Type of client or user.

- ◆ Use of volunteers.

- ◆ Cost effectiveness.

- ◆ Partnerships and collaboration.

OUTCOMES AND ACTIVITIES

Many agencies now use a simple model of inputs, outputs and outcomes to evaluate their work:

Inputs	**The resources** (the money, the time, the people) **committed to an activity.**
Activities	**The services provided.** Examples include a training course, an information service or campaign.
Outputs	**What and how much gets produced or delivered.** Usually expressed through quantitative measures such as "250 hours of training delivered".
Outcomes	**The difference made.** What are the short and long term benefits of the activity? Does it meet the need?

Most people now recognise that simply undertaking activities and producing outputs without checking on the outcomes is not a productive or sensible use of time and limited resources. Outcomes are hard to identify, often outside of an organisation's direct control and may not be seen for some considerable time. However, outcomes are really what an organisation was set up to achieve and why it should continue to exist.

However well managed, activities and outputs without outcomes are pointless. As management writer, Peter Drucker said, "There is nothing so useless as doing efficiently that which should not be done at all".

Recent work on this, in particular an American book, Outcome Funding, by Harold S. Williams and Arthur Y Webb challenges traditional ways of planning, funding and measuring our work. It suggests that our starting point should be the identification of possible outcomes. Measures and milestones towards the outcome can also be identified. Charting these points along the way will allow progress towards the desired outcomes to be monitored. An organisation can then use a range of activities to move towards the outcomes.

Examples of outcomes include:

◆ "Enabling a person to continue to live independently".

◆ "Establishing a self-help group capable of running its own affairs and sustaining itself".

◆ "Recruiting and supporting a trained volunteer network".

Most organisational systems such as job titles, job descriptions and structures are geared around the activity rather than the outcome. Often the energy needed to keep the activity going can start to obscure the outcome. Giving advice, providing a day centre and running a training centre are descriptions of activity and not outcome.

A useful exercise in a planning session is to work through a three stage process:

◆ What outcomes do we wish to achieve?

◆ What are the indicators for each outcome and milestones towards its achievement?

◆ What are the activities that will help us achieve the outcome?

DRAWING UP A MISSION STATEMENT

Informed by work on what drives the organisation, what makes it unique and what outcomes are important, you should now be able to produce a short mission (or vision) statement for your organisation that sets out its purpose. Good mission statements:

◆ Are short. No more than forty words.

◆ Are focused on the value to the user and the relationship with the user.

◆ Set out the overarching goal of the organisation.

◆ Describes the values that will influence how that goal will be achieved.

Mission statements do not need to be measurable, specific or targeted. A mission statement by itself is useless. Once agreed it must be followed up by a clear strategy for the organisation and focused objectives for its work.

CATERING OR CARE

The Millhead charity provided meals on wheels for isolated elderly people living alone. The charity had expanded rapidly over the past few years and had appointed a coordinator to lead a dedicated team of staff and volunteers. The coordinator was soon involved in negotiating contracts with social services and producing the never ending documentation that the social services department demanded.

A year into the post, the coordinator organised a review day with staff, trustees and volunteers. This review session looked at the new quality assurance standards developed at the instigation of social services. They set out various minimum standards about menu choice, food nutrition and catering management. Somehow they did not feel right.

At the end of the session it suddenly occurred to the coordinator that the activity of cooking and delivering food had taken over from the charity's original purpose, to support, care for and befriend isolated elderly people. The means had become the end.

The coordinator explained her feelings to the group. A volunteer said that what was important to the old people she was delivering meals to was knowing that the same person would visit them every Tuesday and Thursday lunchtime and not how often the menu changed or how healthy the meal was. Another talked about how for some old people the actual meal was pretty irrelevant, but what was important was the five minutes of conversation with the volunteer.

After the session the coordinator worked on a business plan that stressed that what the charity valued was personal care and time with elderly people. These aims could be delivered in a several ways such as home visiting, good neighbour schemes or helping relatives to visit more often as well as delivering food.

The mission statement shifted the focus from providing a catering service to a service providing individual care and contact delivered through a variety of activities.

THE LANGUAGE OF BUSINESS PLANNING

The Mission
The overarching goal, purpose and values of the organisation. The big picture.

Strategic Aims
Key priorities and direction for the organisation over the medium to short-term.

Critical Success Factors
Ingredients that the organisation needs to get right to achieve the plan.

Operational Objectives
Measurable, detailed action plans listing the tasks needed to meet the aims.

WORKING OUT A MISSION STATEMENT

The following eight points are useful in working out a mission statement:

❶ OBJECTS
What are the objects and purpose of your organisation as set out in the constitution?

----

❷ ORIGINAL VISION
What was your organisation's original vision, purpose or function?

----

❸ CHANGING CIRCUMSTANCES
How has that changed? What parts of it are still relevant?

----

❹ NEW REQUIREMENTS
What needs to be added to bring it up to date?

----

❺ CENTRAL PURPOSE
What should now be the overriding purpose and direction? What threads hold it together?

----

❻ RATIONALE FOR CONTINUING
Why does the organisation continue to exist?

WORKING OUT A MISSION STATEMENT

CURRENT VALUES 7
What values hold the organisation together?

IDENTITY AND 8 POSITION
What should be the organisation's identity?
How does this relate to other organisations fulfilling similar or complementary functions?

REVIEW YOUR ANSWERS

Try to identify key themes. Now try to draft a mission statement. Keep it to between thirty and forty words.

IS THERE A NEED FOR STRATEGIC THINKING

The following eight statements were made by a group of managers about to embark on a strategic planning exercise.

Do any of these sentiments sound like your organisation's ?

	YES	NO

❶ "We have grown far too fast. Some parts of the organisation are now disconnected from each other".

COMMENTS

❷ "We are drifting. For the past few years all our energy has been spent on keeping going. We need to establish a new direction".

COMMENTS

❸ "We need to establish a common sense of purpose and direction that will hold the project together".

COMMENTS

❹ "We could be criticised for trying to be all things to all people. We need to sort out our identity and make priorities".

COMMENTS

IS THERE A NEED FOR STRATEGIC THINKING

	YES	NO

3 "The need for our services is growing fast, the resources to meet that need are declining. We are in danger of becoming a crisis, "first aid" service". ☐ ☐

COMMENTS

6 "We have been so busy managing that we have missed out on several opportunities to develop new initiatives". ☐ ☐

COMMENTS

7 "I have trouble explaining what the organisation is for to outsiders". ☐ ☐

COMMENTS

8 "We are in danger of becoming complacent and inward looking. We can not assume that what we are doing now will be the same in two years time." ☐ ☐

COMMENTS

GATHERING INFORMATION

> **Get the facts first.**
>
> **You can always distort them later.**
>
> MARK TWAIN

A business plan must include a realistic assessment of the following:

◆ Basic management information about the cost of the service and organisational performance.

◆ A review of likely future trends and scenarios.

◆ A critical appraisal of the organisation's strengths and weaknesses.

The business plan needs to demonstrate that past history and current performance have been properly evaluated to create the best plan for the future. This chapter looks at how organisations can collect and interpret information and feed it into a plan.

Broadly speaking, the information you need can be divided into three categories:

❶ EXTERNAL DEVELOPMENTS

The state of the organisation's "market".
New ways of working and new developments in the sector.
New needs and new types of users.
Developments in similar agencies and statutory provision.
Known factors that will require a response.
Predicted factors and trends that could require a response.

❷ INTERNAL DEVELOPMENTS

Recognition of key strengths and weaknesses of the organisation.
Recognition of key strengths and weaknesses of the services provided.
The extent of need.
The quality of the service.
Estimates of how the service being provided will develop.
The needs and expectations of current users.

❸ FINANCIAL ISSUES

What it costs to operate.
How your costs compare to other agencies.
Financial income trends.
Break even and break points.
Cost effectiveness in relation to outcomes as well as outputs.

USING A SWOT ANALYSIS TO GET STARTED

A SWOT exercise is a useful starting point for a planning session. In the SWOT exercise, participants record under each heading how they currently see the organisation (its strength and its weaknesses) and how they see its future (opportunities that could arise and threats that may need to be faced). In using a SWOT exercise the following things often happen:

◆ People often find it easier to list weaknesses and threats than strengths and opportunities. It is often useful to insist that each participant identifies a minimum number of strengths.

A very well established tool in business planning is a SWOT exercise. It involves participants in identifying and recording:

- **STRENGTHS**
- **WEAKNESSES**
- **OPPORTUNITIES**
- **THREATS**

◆ What some people see as a weakness others might see as a strength. One person might describe a day centre as being disorganised and "not professional" while someone else might see it as being flexible, informal and accessible to clients. Discussion of such different and seemingly contradictory perspectives can be very valuable.

◆ Often things are neither an opportunity or a threat. They move around in the middle. A voluntary group might see the change from grant aid to a service contract as something that "could go either way". A useful question that leads into strategic planning is "what do we need to do to make sure that it is a positive opportunity?".

◆ People often spend most of their time focussing on what they can do to overcome their weaknesses. However, it is often worthwhile to spend time on the strengths list and identify the critical factors that lead to something being a strength and importantly, what does the organisation need to do to keep something a strength and build on it.

A SWOT analysis can be a useful tool for presenting information in a business plan.

PREDICTING FUTURE TRENDS

Our ability to predict accurately how things will be in the next few years is very limited. Traditional planners have tried to sift information and make accurate forecasts of the future. They are usually not very accurate and occasionally downright wrong! The approach outlined here is more about predicting trends, identifying possible actions needed and agreeing contingencies. Strategic management is about having a clear direction to steer towards and at the same time being able to respond to new developments and changes.

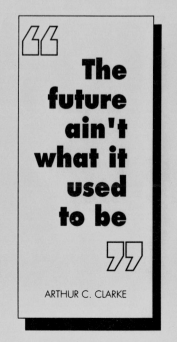

The future ain't what it used to be

ARTHUR C. CLARKE

The following five headings are useful to work through to identify future trends:

❶ Changes in available resources

What will happen to resources (human, physical and financial) that we currently have? How will our income be affected?

❷ Changes in how we work

How might the working methods and styles change? How will practices change? What is new in our field?

❸ Changes in demands and needs

What will happen to our current user base? How might our user profile change? Will demand for our service go up or down?

❹ Changes in the political/economic arena

What could be the impact of new legislation, changes in policy direction and the state of the economy?

❺ Changes in the environment and market

What will happen to other agencies with which we work? Will we cooperate or compete?

PREDICTING FUTURE TRENDS AND DEVELOPMENTS

	AVAILABLE RESOURCES	CHANGES IN HOW WE WORK	CHANGES IN DEMAND & NEEDS	POLITICAL/ECONOMIC CHANGES	CHANGES IN ENVIRONMENT/MARKET
NEXT 12 MONTHS	Fund raising from public will stand still or decline	Some services at breaking point if demand continues		How will community care reforms work in practice & impact on us?	Do we cooperate or compete with similar agencies?
1-3 YEARS	Lease expires on building 12.96 End of three year funding for development post	External evaluation of project scheduled Active development of user groups	Impact of recession on users and carers	Move to a new local authority structure	Push for a formal quality assurance system
LONGER TERM	Move to contracts rather than grants Unable to predict past three years!	Long term aim of user control and management	Our clients will get older...break up of care arrangements Greater demands for choice and independence	Voluntary agencies having to take over previous statutory services	Potential conflict with other providers over values

A voluntary organisation working with people with learning disabilities produced this chart which scanned possible changes in its environment. They then went on to identify how these events and trends could be responded to in their business planning process.

After completing a similar exercise for your organisation - *use the worksheet on page 34* - it is useful to note the factors which are definite, which are probable and which are possible. It might be useful to to see if any themes or links emerge between the different factors.

A further exercise - *on page 35* - is to look at how the organisation fits

LOOKING OUTSIDE

A locally managed housing advice project carried out this exercise to look at how it related to other agencies who did similar work to it. The following chart is a summary of their analysis:

AGENCY	SIMILARITIES	DIFFERENCES & STRENGTHS	RELATIONSHIP	STRATEGIC ISSUES
Citizens Advice Bureau.	Open door policy. Very busy.	Part of a national service. Deals with more issues than housing. Better public profile. Uses volunteers.	Good cooperation. Some joint training.	Potential for more Joint work.
Law Centre.	Very busy.	Appointments only Qualified staff. More specialist.	Lost contact due to staff changes.	Need to establish contact. Will they continue to do housing cases?
Housing Aid Centre at Town Hall.	Only works in housing. Open door.	Directly managed by Council. We are independent. They are better resourced.	Poor relationship in the past.	Could we be rivals for funding? Do we overlap? How can we work together?
Solicitors in private practice.		They are profit making. Expensive. We are a free service.	Little contact. except when they act for landlords!	As recession hits private firms might move into this area?

into organisations doing similar work. This can be useful to predict potential conflicts, identify possible problems and possibly future alliances.

Looking outside at what others are doing might identify some of the following:

◆ Potential for joint working, cooperation, alliances or even mergers.

◆ By looking at others it might help you to identify what is unique about the service and so help in marketing and fund raising efforts.

◆ It might identify some potential conflicts, most obviously for funds, that may need planning for.

The next stage is to agree a strategy that will respond to the external world and allow some flexibility.
Sources of information about external trends might include:

◆ Government statistics (eg. Social Trends, Household Trends).

◆ Local Authority data on demographic trends.

◆ Community Care plans.

◆ Research by your own agency and other agencies.

◆ Discussions with funders about their plans.

◆ Information from clients, obtained formally and informally.

PREDICTING INTERNAL TRENDS

It is often quite hard to take stock of how the organisation has developed to date, its current performance and significant factors that might affect its future. Often people working in the organisation can be too close to it to see anything objectively. Changes often happen gradually over time and are absorbed without conscious thought.

Good strategic planning needs to include (and make reference to in the business plan) some evaluation of the organisation as it now is.

It is useful to divide this into two categories:

❶ Reviewing the organisation's "programme"
The programme comprises of the activities, services and projects of the organisation. Programme evaluation asks; Are we meeting needs? Do the services meet our objectives? How effective are we?

❷ Reviewing the organisation's "process"
Process is the ways of working that an organisation has in place to meet its task. Do the structures, systems and ways of working help or hinder the organisation in meeting its goals?

In looking at these issues it is important that the mission of the organisation is clear.

The review has to be in a context of what the organisation stands for. This provides a basis for agreeing a criteria by which programmes and processes can be evaluated.

It is also valuable to involve others in this activity. Users, carers, partners and sometimes funders can provide a useful insight and stop the exercise becoming one of self-justification.

Products often go through a life cycle described as:

REVIEWING THE PROGRAMME

In the world of marketing, the idea of a product life cycle is often used to plan how long a particular brand will remain profitable.

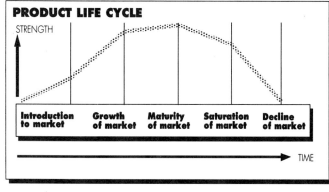

PRODUCT LIFE CYCLE

STRENGTH

| Introduction to market | Growth of market | Maturity of market | Saturation of market | Decline of market |

TIME

Commentators have noted how services and products now tend to move through this cycle much more quickly. It is likely that a "state of the art" computer purchased today will be out of date and need to be replaced by another machine within twelve months. In the middle of 1992, a senior manager at Apple Computers estimated that half of its' turnover in 1993 would come from seventy products that had not at that stage been introduced to the market.

Such a rate of change can be very frustrating for managers. As voluntary organisations increasingly operate on a shorter time span and as funding becomes more targeted to the latest "new" idea, a feeling of "change for changes sake" can quickly develop. The danger of simply responding to current "flavour of the month" and jumping from one idea or project to another is real. However, it is useful to ask the following questions:

◆ *If we were designing the organisation from scratch, would it have the same services and the same activities as it has today?*

◆ *What drives the service? Is it really led by user needs, or is it mainly based on "the way that we have always done things"?*

◆ *What will each service look like in a few years time? What resources will it need to operate?*

A PORTFOLIO ANALYSIS

A useful planning tool is to try to look at an organisation as a collection - or portfolio - of different activities, projects and services. You can then make sure that there is an appropriate balance amongst the activities or projects.

A popular technique used by commercial organisations is the "growth share matrix" developed by the Boston Consulting Group. With a little adaption, it can also be used by voluntary agencies.

The matrix is divided into four squares:

Square one: The stars of an organisation. These are the activities and services that are particularly strong and have real potential for growth. They are often dynamic, popular and creative. Stars can often fall or turn out to be short lived "shooting stars".

Square two: The question marks or problem children. New activities that take up resources , but, as yet, produce little return. They are often new or innovative projects that might become stars and move onto square one and really work or fail and move into square four.

Square three: The cash cows. The reliable, safe services and products that have an entrenched position and provide a degree of security. They provide a solid base for the organisation.

Square four: The "dogs" and "dead ducks". These are the

activities that take up resources and effort and produce little value in return. Often organisations have problems extricating themselves from such activities.

From working with the model several strategic choices and options may be identified:

What criteria are being used? A financial perspective might see an activity as being in square three in that it can bring in lots of income; whereas someone committed to service development might see it in square four as it is taking up a lot of time just to keep it running.

What should be the balance? What sort of balance do we need between dynamic and risky projects and steady and stable ones? How much effort and time do we put into research and development? What should be the balance between things that work well now and how they will work in the future?

How do activities move between boxes? The activities placed in square four (dead ducks/dogs) may at one time have been your stars. How can managers help services move through the matrix and recognise that at some point difficult decisions about their future may be needed?

STRATEGIC QUESTIONS TO ASK

Strategic questions to ask about the services placed in each box:

❶ The Stars

- ◆ Why is it a star?
- ◆ What are the factors that have placed it in this box?
- ◆ How can we replicate these factors elsewhere?
- ◆ How long will it be a star for?
- ◆ Where will it go next?

❷ Question marks or problem children

- ◆ How long does this activity need to prove itself?
- ◆ How will we know when it is successful?
- ◆ How do we manage risk, innovation and possible failure?

❸ Cash cows

- ◆ Will this activity stay steady and stable?
- ◆ Is there a danger of taking it for granted?

❹ Dogs and dead ducks

- ◆ Do we close it down or renew it?
- ◆ What would be the cost of closing this down?
- ◆ Why have we let it move into this box?

CASE STUDY-YOUTH DEVELOPMENT AGENCY
• PORTFOLIO MATRIX •

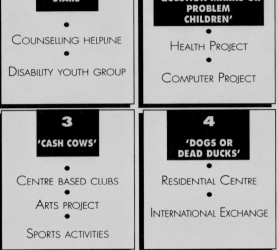

1	2
'STARS'	**'QUESTION MARKS OR PROBLEM CHILDREN'**
• COUNSELLING HELPLINE • DISABILITY YOUTH GROUP	• HEALTH PROJECT • COMPUTER PROJECT

3	4
'CASH COWS'	**'DOGS OR DEAD DUCKS'**
• CENTRE BASED CLUBS • ARTS PROJECT • SPORTS ACTIVITIES	• RESIDENTIAL CENTRE • INTERNATIONAL EXCHANGE

Square 1 consisted of two new projects that were "breaking new ground" locally, were picking up considerable media interest and were getting a very good response from young people who the project had traditionally very little relationship with. One of the projects, the counselling line, was also attracting interest from a neighbouring local authority who expressed an interest in developing a similar service.

Square 2 had two projects. A health project that was still very much at a pilot stage. No-one knew if it would work, but, it was considered worth investing in. The computer project had been around the organisation for two years. It had attracted little interest from users (or funders) and really was little more than a "pipe dream" of a particular worker.

Square 3 took up most of the organisation's resources. They were the main activities that operated on a week to week basis. Over the past five years they had changed little and as far as the organisation was concerned would continue to serve a useful purpose. One of the activities, the arts project, was causing concern. It was starting to drift. It was attracting fewer young people. It's funder had described it as "becoming rather predictable".

Square 4 had two activities that were part of the agency's history. The residential centre, a cottage, was donated to the agency ten years ago. At that time it was, for a short period, a "star". For the past two years it had needed considerable repairs, a new roof and regular visits from the agency's administrator. As a result, it drained resources and because of the poor state of repair few groups ever visited. The international exchange programme had become an annual commitment that the agency did "because it had done it last year". Few people participated, it often went over budget and took up considerable staff time. However, those who did participate thought that it was very valuable.

The portfolio analysis highlighted six strategic choices for the agency.

❶ Innovation was seen as an important role for the agency. How much time and money could we risk in square 2? How much time should we give new ideas to establish themselves?

❷ What future is there for the two items in square 1? Could they peak? What if funders lost interest (moved onto other stars), but, expectation from users continued to rise?

❸ Are we really confident that the items in square 3 are steady and safe?

❹ What do we need to do with the arts project? How do we stop it drifting into square 4?

❺ What future do we envisage for the residential centre? Do we invest in it, market it and give it a new direction or do we look to dispose of it?

❻ Should we continue with the international exchanges? If we move out of this area will we get opposition from those of our members who benefit from it? Could we float it off to someone more skilled in this area?

REVIEWING THE PROCESS

An important question to ask in any strategic plan is how does the way that we are organised "fit" with what it is we want to do?

Over time, organisations develop procedures, systems and structures for organising their activities. It is easy for job descriptions, departmental structures and internal processes to become restrictive and prevent an organisation changing or thinking strategically.

Often the system can take on a life of its own. A manager employed by a housing agency to develop community based initiatives analysed how her time was being spent. She was alarmed to find that over 50% of her time was spent on dealing with the structure that employed her. Attending and servicing meetings, filling in paperwork, responding to requests for information and "playing the system" seemed more important than her actual job.

In a planning exercise it is useful to focus on three issues:

❶ Is the organisation flexible enough to respond to the changes and uncertainties that we have to deal with?

❷ Does the way we are organised "fit" with our task and our values?

❸ Do all aspects of the organisation work together?

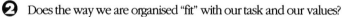

The management consultancy firm, McKinsey & Company, developed a useful framework for taking stock of how an entity organises itself. They argued that for an organisation to work effectively, it had to achieve a "synergy" between seven elements, all of which helpfully began with the letter **S**.

S▶① STRATEGY
- ◆ Does the organisation have a clear purpose?
- ◆ Is it future orientated?
- ◆ Do people in it understand its strategy?

S▶② STRUCTURE
- ◆ Does the way that work is divided up make sense?
- ◆ Is the structure flexible enough?
- ◆ Does it allow good communication between people?

S▶③ STAFF
- ◆ Are the right sort of people in the right sort of jobs?
- ◆ What sort of employer are we?

S▶④ SKILLS
- ◆ Do we have the right skill mix to develop in the way we want to?
- ◆ Are there any current skills gaps in the organisation?
- ◆ How do we invest in the staff that we currently have?

S▶⑤ SYSTEMS
- ◆ Do we have sufficient management control over our resources?
- ◆ Do we know what things cost?
- ◆ How do we make decisions?

S▶⑥ STYLE
- ◆ What is our relationship to our users like?
- ◆ Do we present the kind of image that we want to?

S▶⑦ SHARED VALUES
- ◆ Are the organisation's shared values clear?
- ◆ Is there a clear agreement about what is important?
- ◆ Is there a clear agreement about how we work?

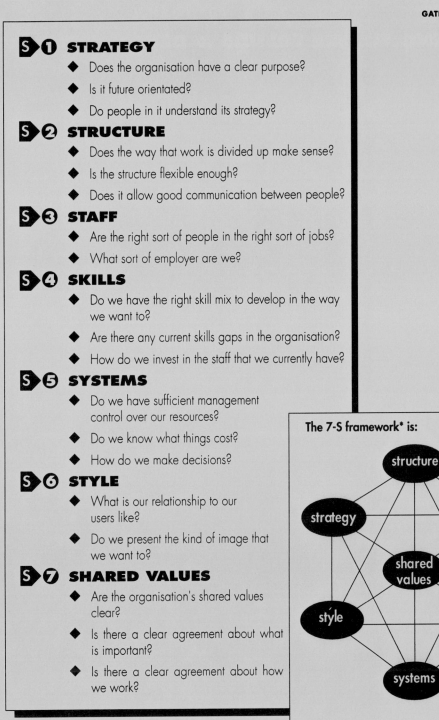

The 7-S framework* is:

The 7-S framework can be used to identify weaknesses and shortcomings in how an organisation works.

* Copyright © 1980 Mckinsey & Company, Inc. Reproduced by permission.

33

PREDICTING FUTURE TRENDS & DEVELOPMENTS

	NEXT 12 MONTHS	1-3 YEARS	LONGER TERM
AVAILABLE RESOURCES			
CHANGES IN HOW WE WORK			
CHANGES IN DEMAND & NEEDS			
POLITICAL /ECONOMIC CHANGES			
CHANGES IN ENVIRONMENT /MARKET			

LOOKING OUTSIDE

List all the organisations who do similar work to you. Include organisations in the voluntary, public and private sectors as appropriate. Note what is similar and what is different. What are their particular strengths? Consider the following issues:

◆ What will the future relationship between your and their organisations be? Cooperative or competitive?

◆ Are there any opportunities for joint work and alliances?

◆ Are there dangers of rivalry or other threats?

ORGANISATION	SIMILARITIES	DIFFERENCES & STRENGTHS	RELATIONSHIP	STRATEGIC ISSUES

DOING A SWOT ANALYSIS

Set out the strengths and weaknesses of the organganisation as you see them. Note possible opportunities and threats which may emerge in the future.

STRENGTHS

WEAKNESSES

OPPORTUNITIES

THREATS

PORTFOLIO ANALYSIS

Amongst the work of your organisation you will be able to identify projects with different characteristics which contribute in different ways to the organisation's personality and future development. These can be classified in four broad categories:

① **Stars:** strong projects with real potential for growth, dynamic, popular and creative.

② **Question marks or problem children:** new or innovative projects, but not yet proven.

③ **Cash cows:** reliable, safe services that provide the organisation with a degree of security.

④ **Dogs and dead ducks:** take up management and financial resources and provide little value for the effort involved.

Place your organisation's services and projects on the Boston portfolio matrix by allocating each one to one of the four squares:

Now answer the following questions:
◆ Is the balance of the portfolio right?

- -

- -

- -

- -

◆ How will each of the projects develop over the next year or so? (consider likely demand, trends and income).

- -

- -

- -

◆ How do we manage activities in squares 1 & 2?

- -

- -

- -

◆ How do we manage activities in squares 3 & 4?

- -

- -

- -

1 'STARS'	**2** 'QUESTION MARKS OR PROBLEM CHILDREN'

3 'CASH COWS'	**4** 'DOGS OR DEAD DUCKS'

SORTING OUT THE NUMBERS

Some business plans consist of little more than financial projections. There has been a tendency, particularly from banks, to ask that the business plan projects income for the next three years, gives a detailed cash flow analysis and shows that the business is (and will remain in years to come) a safe and viable concern.

This is often a pointless exercise. Few organisations in any sector can accurately predict their financial position much beyond the next financial year.

However, a business plan needs to show the following:

◆ That the organisation is **financially viable** and that it has thought through its financial policy and likely income and expenditure in an intelligent and realistic way.

◆ That it has made **sensible assumptions** about it's likely financial future.

◆ That it has **realistically costed** its activities and taken into account the need for **contingencies**.

◆ That it has sufficient **financial controls** to properly manage and plan.

◆ That it has coherent **financial management** policies.

Increasingly investors are more interested in the assumptions behind a plan. This involves checking that the financial plan has been properly considered rather than checking every item of anticipated income and expenditure line by line.

This chapter looks at six issues:

❶ What **financial information** do you need?

❷ How can you **forecast income?**

❸ Establishing the **break-even point** & the **break point**.

❹ Establishing **what an activity costs**.

❺ Forecasting **cash flow**.

❻ A checklist of **ten financial questions** to consider.

WHAT FINANCIAL INFORMATION DO YOU NEED?

Many voluntary organisations have delegated financial management entirely to the treasurer or finance officer. It has been their job to manage the "bottom line", to look after the budget, to keep the organisation solvent and to ensure that reports are produced annually to meet constitutional and legal requirements. Due to changes in the regulatory environment (the 1992 and 1993 Charities Act), changing funding patterns and increased requirements from funders, more attention is being paid to financial management and all trustees and managers are being expected to participate in financial decision making. The increased emphasis on financial management is important for three good reasons:

1 The harsher economic & funding climate means that many organisations are facing difficult financial choices.

2 Contracts and service agreements require an organisation to accurately cost and price individual projects and services. In the past statutory bodies made a grant aid contribution to support an organisation. Contracting is about purchasing a specific service from an organisation at a pre-determined price. If the price is wrong the service still has to be delivered.

3 Greater public scrutiny of voluntary organisations is expected. The Charity Commission's SORP (new accounting practice) will create greater clarity in accounts.

This chart describes five main sources of financial information that most voluntary agencies will have.

	WHAT IT IS FOR	WHAT SHOULD IT TELL YOU?	HOW YOU CAN USE IT?
THE BUDGET 1	An estimate of income and expenditure for a set period, usually a year.	Where the money should go & where it should come from.	Regular (usually monthly or at least quarterly) reports will show actual income and spending compared to the budget.
THE BALANCE SHEET 2	A snapshot of the financial health of the organisation on a particular day. Usually the year end.	The current value of the organisation i.e. the difference between liabilities (money owed) and its assets (what it owns (fixed and current)).	The "acid test" of viability. Is the organisation a going concern?
THE RECEIPTS & PAYMENTS ACCOUNT 3	What cash was received and what cash was paid out in a period.	How the organisation is spending and receiving money.	To reconcile spending with the bank account and to monitor cash flow.
THE INCOME & EXPENDITURE ACCOUNT 4	The receipts & payments account adjusted to include money owed to it and owed by it. To give a true picture of the organisation's income and spending.	Will income meet expenditure?	The current financial performance.
CASH FLOW FORECAST 5	Timed forecast of when income will be received compared with planned spending.	Are there any points when there will not be enough cash to meet outgoing?	Use it to ensure scheduling of income and expenditure.

A business plan will usually include summaries of the main financial reports. How they are presented will depend on two things:

❶ How open you wish to be about your organisation's financial affairs. For example, some organisations negotiating contracts have felt in a weaker position because their potential purchasers have had full details of their financial arrangements.

❷ Your ability to be accurate about future financial projections. The further you plan from the present, the less certain your financial projections will be. One organisation produced draft income and expenditure forecasts on the following basis.

◆ **YEAR ONE:** Monthly projections.

◆ **YEAR TWO:** Quarterly estimates.

◆ **YEAR THREE:** A rough estimate of income and expenditure for the year.

HOW CAN YOU PROJECT INCOME?

Many organisations are plagued by the short term outlook of some funders. It is easy to get caught up in an April to April scramble for cash. An essential activity in a business plan is to try to predict income trends in future years.

Possible income sources might include:

◆ Grant aid from statutory bodies.

◆ Service agreements and contracts.

◆ Grants from trusts and companies.

◆ Public fund raising.

◆ Sponsorship.

◆ Legacies.

◆ Subscriptions and donations from members.

◆ Profit from trading operations.

◆ Earned income from the sale of services.

◆ Hire of resources.

◆ Investment income.

◆ Management fees.

◆ Consultancy fees.

◆ Income from users (such as rent).

The process of analysing these income sources is often called a "sensitivity analysis" in the jargon of business planning. This should consist of three elements:

❶ Reviewing current position. How stable has the income been in the past?

❷ How do we predict each source of income developing? What is likely to happen to it? What is it dependent on? How reliable will it be?

❸ What action is needed to achieve the target? What can we do to secure this income? How can we protect or extend it through better marketing or better negotiating?

ESTABLISHING THE BREAK-EVEN POINT & BREAK POINT

In any profit making venture the break-even point and the break point are of critical concern. The break-even point is the point at which income from trading starts to overtake the fixed and variable costs of the operation.

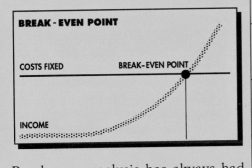

Break-even analysis has always had relevance when a service receives income for every time it gets used. For example, a hostel needs to fill so many beds each night to remain viable. For some, identifying the break-even and break point might not be so straightforward.

PREDICTING TRENDS IN CURRENT INCOME

A community arts agency produced the following prediction of its likely sources of income for the next three years.

INCOME	CURRENT POSITION	PREDICTION OF TRENDS	ACTION NEEDED
Council grant from Leisure Committee.	30% of income. Annually agreed. Use not specified.	Will evolve into service agreement. Will probably stay at same level or inflation plus.	Push for three year agreement. Sort out a negotiating strategy.
Regional Arts Board (RAB) funding.	25% of income. Annually agreed for running costs.	Review by RAB to be carried out this year.	Follow up review. Monitor (RAB's) changing funding criteria.
Commercial sponsorship for Artist in Residence.	14% of income. Will end this year.	We will lose a management fee of £2,000.	Identify actual loss to central costs. Alternative funding?
Fee earned for local estate work.	12% of income from 4 "contracts".	Difficult to predict. Do they cost more than we think?	Need marketing outside of current network. Review pricing policy.
Hire of building for events.	9% of income.	Bookings falling from previous year's level.	Need to review this area. Need to market it.
Office rented to outside group.	6% of income.	Not a realistic rent level.	Schedule rent review.
Donations. Miscellaneous income.	4% of income.	Will probably stay at this level with minimal effort.	Do we need a fund raising strategy?

This activity quickly identified some issues for the management to address:

◆ Does it really know what each activity costs?
◆ Did it properly cost out the full cost of a project or activity before taking it on?

One interesting aspect of this exercise was that no individual in the agency had responsibility for managing specific income. Hire of the building, office rent, donations and sponsorship were all organised on a very ad hoc basis. No one thought about them in a strategic way, but, they accounted for 31% of the agency's income.

• CASE STUDY•

THE COMMUNITY CAFE'S BREAK-EVEN & BREAK POINTS

A community cafe calculated that they would have to meet a fixed cost of £85 each week regardless of how many meals they sold. The fixed costs would include rent, wages and payments on hire purchase. As the chart below shows, even if the cafe sells no meals it still has to pay out £85 in fixed costs. The variable cost is 40p for every meal it makes. This is the additional cost of every meal it sells at 75p.

At 244 meals the cafe reaches the break-even point. Income from sales has overtaken the combined fixed and variable cost. At 244 meals the cafe moves into profit, the fixed cost remains the same and only the extra variable cost of each meal sold is added to the total cost.

However a point would be reached when the growth of the operation means that the ability to respond to growth is inadequate. At around 400 to 450 meals the cafe starts to hit break point. The cafe needs to invest in more equipment, more space and more staff to cope with increased customer demand. If it fails to do this, it is likely that the service will start to suffer. The quality of both the food and the service will be reduced, staff could become stressed and customers might stop coming. The cafe could be harmed by its own success.

At, or even better, well before, the break point, the cafe needs to have the cash to expand its capacity to do business. This will add to its fixed costs (taking them to £170 per week) and in the example shown takes the cafe (hopefully only temporarily) back into a loss. It could have planned for this by setting aside a certain sum each week to cover such expansion and increased cost.

FIXED COSTS: £85 per week
VARIABLE COST: £0.40 (i.e. cost per meal)
PRICE: £0.75p

MEALS SOLD	FIXED COST	UNIT COST	TOTAL COST	INCOME	PROFIT/ (LOSS)
450	£170	£180	£350	£337.50	(£12.50)
400	£85	£160	£245	£300	£55
300	£85	£120	£205	£225	£20
250	£85	£100	£185	£187.50	£02.50
244	£85	£97.60	£182.60	£183.40	£00.80
200	£85	£80	£165	£150	(£15)
100	£85	£40	£125	£75	(£50)
0	£85	0	£85	0	(£85)

The break point is that point at which the service reaches capacity. New clients can only be dealt with if extra resources (human and physical) are provided. Every organisation has a point where it becomes viable and certainly a point at which if it continues to take on more work it will have gone past its capacity. Beyond the break point it will then start simply responding and crisis managing. It is worth noting that sometimes the most relevant break points are not to do with cash income. They could include staffing levels, casework systems and physical space.

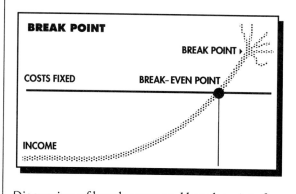

Discussion of break-even and break points for voluntary organisations highlights several important strategic issues.

Many voluntary organisations have a culture that encourages people to go beyond the break point, never say "no" and somehow manage to provide a service to more people with either the same or declining resources. The long term consequence of this is that a service becomes ed only by demand, it only reacts to pressure and sooner or later the quality of work suffers.

The problem of the break point is a problem of success. Demand for the service has outstripped the capacity to supply it. Several studies of small business failures point to growing too fast or growing beyond its capacity as reasons for failure. In many instances managing rapid growth and increasing demand is as hard as managing crisis and decline.

In a profit making enterprise it should be possible

to see the break point approaching, produce a business plan that shows the venture's success and gain the financial backing to obtain extra financial resources to take it over the break point. When a voluntary organisation reaches a break point it is highly unusual for a funding body to offer additional cash because the organisation is very busy. Several agreements between voluntary and statutory agencies are very clear about the minimum service requirements, but are silent about the point at which the service being purchased reaches break point and a further contract would have to be negotiated. Increasingly, strategic management is about identifying the current capacity of the organisation and managing demand in a fair and equitable way.

ESTABLISHING WHAT AN ACTIVITY COSTS

Traditionally, budgeting in voluntary organisations has been about making sure that there will be sufficient income to meet projected expenditure. The focus has been on getting the "bottom line" to balance. Changes in funding arrangements, the increased use of specific projects within organisations and an increased unwillingness to pay for core or admin costs has led several agencies to move away from a traditional budget to one which more accurately shows the full cost of a specific activity.

A traditional budget usually has the following format:

INCOME	EXPENDITURE
Council grant...........	Salaries....................
Trust & company Donations................	Administration........... Building costs............
Subscriptions/ Membership............	Project expenditure ....
Fund raising.............	
Sales income...........	
TOTAL	TOTAL

• CASE STUDY•

MANAGING THE BREAK POINT

The Morton Family Centre was faced with a dilemma. Over the three years it had been open, cases and referrals were rising by about 15% per year. Word of mouth recommendations, successful publicity work and high quality services had contributed to this increased demand.

At the end of the third year, an external evaluation pointed to four issues that needed attention:

1 The centre did no organised follow up work with its clients.

2 Workers were increasingly only dealing with urgent cases, rather than working in a preventative way.

3 Time for staff supervision and development was often lacking. High caseloads often meant that workers were too busy to look after themselves.

4 The centre was starting to only work with families referred through social services. This was often seen as quicker and "more managed", whereas open access work often took up more time.

It was clear that the centre was close to its break point. Client work was becoming less responsive to individual needs, staff were feeling under increasing pressure, waiting time for services had grown to the point where opportunity for early intervention was lost and internal management systems were starting to crack.

The centre's main strategic issue was how to cope with increasing demand with no prospect of increasing resources to cope with it. Two issues were worked on by the staff and management committee:

How to be more effective at saying "no" to new casework. There was a need to manage the intake routes into the centre and in particular explain to agencies who referred clients the limitations of it. To some extent, the internal culture of the centre had to change, people often took on impossible caseloads, because they felt guilty about saying no.

The second issue was to include in the centre's business plan and in all future funding agreements a series of "management ratios" that would make sure that the centre did not go beyond its break point. The ratios included:

◆ Number of clients per caseworker.

◆ Amount of direct time and time for follow up and supervision.

◆ Number of direct workers and available management time.

◆ Amount of time for referred work and time available for new work.

A monthly monitoring meeting would act as an early warning system to see if the break point had been reached on any issue.

The budget does not indicate what each activity or service costs. An alternative method of budgeting is called cost centring or activity based budgeting. Several organisations are moving from a traditional budget to one in which all expenditure is charged to a particular activity or project.

Central to cost centring is the division between direct and indirect costs.

◆ Direct costs are the costs that are only incurred as a direct result of running the particular activity. A project's decision to run education courses would therefore involve the cost of trainers, room hire, course material and probably most of the education officer's time. If it did not run education courses it should not incur these costs.

◆ Indirect costs are the shared organisational costs. They are costs that are difficult to apportion to a specific project or activity. Examples in the case study would be some of the manager's time, some administration costs and some building charges. Increasingly, organisations are finding it hard to obtain separate funding for indirect costs.

Moving to a cost centred budget involves the following steps:

❶ Identifying the cost centres to use. This could be related to income sources or to work functions such as particular projects, activities or geographic areas. The centres used should be clear and distinct areas.

❷ Allocating expenditure that can be directly apportioned to each cost centre. This will include supplies, resources and people's time. This process could be done on the basis of past usage ("on average the rural project uses the minibus for a third of its available time").

❸ Agreeing how the remaining expenditure (the things that cannot easily be allocated to a specific cost centre) should be dealt with. In the case study *(see page 50-52)* a fixed formula was used to divide the indirect costs between centres. (The indirect cost is the cost of having the activity within the organisation) .

Developing a cost centred approach raises several issues.

◆ Many voluntary organisations have been very poor at properly costing their work. The costs of spending or using other peoples money can be high. Often the cost involved in operating and providing good management have not been properly identified, under costed or even ignored. This can easily lead to a long term crisis of struggling to do "quality work on the cheap".

◆ Several organisations who have moved into cost centres have realised that the real cost of an activity is often far more than the grant or contract income that they receive from a statutory authority. This can raise the policy issue of should a voluntary organisation subsidise work carried out for statutory bodies. It also may help negotiators adopt a more assertive approach in future contract discussions. There may be occasions when an organisation takes a strategic decision to take on an activity at below its full cost and either cross subsidise or fund raise to fill the gap. In the past, the lack of any real costing information has meant that organisations have often drifted into activities without any sense of the financial implications.

◆ A negative side effect of cost centres is that it can create an unhelpful competitive tension within the organisation. People in one centre can start complaining that they "are more profitable" than others. This needs careful management. Cost centres provide management information that can help with making priorities and attaching value to activities. The value of an activity will probably be measured in more than financial terms.

◆ In some organisations the issue of what is a reasonable amount to spend on indirect costs as opposed to direct ones has become a controversial one. A hostel manager complained that she had to add on £62,000 to her annual costs to pay for her parent organisation. She doubted if she received anywhere near £62,000 worth of management and central services back in return. In other sectors reducing indirect central costs either through "creative accounting" strategies or through "downsizing" in which central services and jobs have been cut has been pursued zealously. Perhaps a more useful approach is to look at how central services can "add value" to the core projects and activities of the organisation through giving direction, providing support and the delivery of efficient services.

FORECASTING CASH FLOW

Business planners are often inclined to be very enthusiastic about cash flow forecasts as many organisations have learnt a hard lesson that an anticipated cash surplus can easily be blown away by budgeted income not arriving on time. Cash flow forecasting is about ensuring that there will always be sufficient cash in a bank account to meet anticipated expenditure.

In reality it is very difficult to predict accurately exact income and expenditure patterns and cash inflows and outflows for more than eighteen months ahead. However, a business plan needs to show the following:

◆ That the impact of cash flow has been considered.

◆ That cash flow will be managed.

◆ That the organisation will have sufficient reserves of working capital to meet its needs.

◆ That the organisation understands its patterns of cash flow including seasonal ups and downs.

In looking at a cash flow forecast it is useful to consider the following questions:

◆ Are there any points at which we will not have sufficient cash to meet our outgoings?

◆ What is our minimum monthly operating cost?

◆ How much working capital do we need to pay for expansion and development?

◆ What could we quickly do to improve our cash flow position in an emergency?

MANAGING CASH FLOW

A business plan may indicate the steps taken to manage and improve cash flow. Tactics might include:

◆ Writing payment schedules (possibly with penalty clauses) into contracts.

◆ Monitoring payment of fees and grants.

◆ Tighter control of people who owe you money.

◆ Faster invoicing.

◆ Spreading out expenditure in instalments.

◆ Delaying some expenditure.

◆   Delaying payment of certain bills.

◆   Better banking arrangements.

A CHECK LIST OF TEN STRATEGIC FINANCIAL QUESTIONS TO CONSIDER

The following ten strategic financial questions are useful in appraising an organisation's financial arrangements and financial strategy as part of the business planning process:

❶ Do we have sufficient working capital?

Working capital is calculated by subtracting current liabilities from current assets. On a balance sheet, this is usually called net current assets. Every organisation needs sufficient working capital to ensure that cash flow can be managed, to develop new projects and to cope with unexpected events. Several voluntary organisations live on a hand to mouth existence where the slightest financial problem can cause a crisis. Many organisations have not been able to follow up opportunities due to a lack of working capital.

❷ Do we know what it costs to operate?

Increasingly, organisations are having to develop accurate costing systems that identify the true cost of a specific activity or service. Costing needs to be accurate and realistic. It should fully take into account both direct and indirect costs and provide regular information that will ensure proper cost control.

❸ How do we price our work?

The cost of an activity should be based on rational facts. The price that a service is offered at is usually based on a tactical or marketing decision.

PRICING YOUR WORK

Three possible strategies for pricing work are available:

❶ PLUS COST

The cost is "marked up" by a fixed percentage to create some surplus and possibly also to allow some room for negotiation with purchasers.

❷ UNDER COST

The fee agreed is below the actual cost. The organisation takes on a piece of work in the full knowledge that it will need to subsidise it. Possible reasons include: to attract future work; because the organisation's cash flow demands cash at any cost, or because the organisation is so committed to the activity that it is prepared to invest its own money in it. There may be occasions when an organisation does take on work under cost, but, it needs to have very clear reasons for doing so.

❸ THE PRICE IS SET BY THE MARKET

There is a "going rate" or an agreed rate for the activity set by the purchaser or by other organisations. The organisation needs to see if it can recover its costs (or even create a surplus) within the price that has already been set.

④ Can we control the patterns of cash flow?

Managing cash flow is important. Ensuring that future funding arrangements take cash flow into account, scheduling income and expenditure, agreeing payment schedules, can all help to overcome potential cash flow problems.

⑤ How much does it cost to use other people's money?

The resistance of some funders to contribute to indirect costs or overheads has meant that the true cost of operating has sometimes been ignored. Some organisations have taken on projects where the income only meets the direct costs. The cost of having the project in the organisation is ignored.

⑥ Is the balance between direct and indirect costs right?

Getting the right balance between project costs and organisational costs can be hard. Some organisations suffer from having an overstaffed and over resourced centre and an under resourced front line. What is a reasonable balance between the centre and the projects? Is the centre too large for the current level of project activity? Does it add value to the project work?

⑦ Are we managing our income as well as our expenditure?

Most organisations have controls over their expenditure that stop them going over budget. Is income also managed? Is sufficient attention paid to ensuring that income keeps to target, that shortfalls are picked up early, and that the future sources of income are carefully researched and managed?

⑧ What sort of contingency fund do we need?

A contingency fund is an essential part of any good financial arrangement. Contingency funds cover unexpected cash flow problems and unforeseen events and circumstances. There has sometimes been a resistance to building one up.

⑨ How will we replace capital items that depreciate over time?

Most capital items lose value over time. Each year the vehicles or equipment that the organisation owns reduce in value. On a balance sheet this is known as depreciation. The rate of depreciation depends on how long the item is expected to last, a proportion is written off every year and some funds should be allocated to a fund to replace the asset at the end of its useful life. It is useful to check that there is sufficient money in the replacement fund to meet likely replacement costs and that the depreciation timetable is accurate. One computer training centre found out that their accountant had assumed that their computers would be replaced every ten years, when it was likely that they would last for three years at the very most. Money needs also to be set aside for repairs, refurbishment and decoration.

⑩ Do we have sufficient financial skills?

Do the in house financial people (treasurer, finance officer) have full control and are they able to provide regular and accurate monitoring information? Are the external financial advisers (eg. accountant or auditor) useful in financial planning and aware of tax, VAT and investment issues?

O O O O O O O O O

CASESTUDY

A TALE OF TWO CULTURES

In the space of two weeks, the Director of a community project had two different discussions about her agency's financial policy.

The voluntary sector liaison officer at the local authority told her that "concern was being expressed" within the authority that the project's recently published annual report had shown an "operating surplus" of £7,000. The project had decided to build up a reserve fund equivalent to six weeks operating costs to cover cash flow, develop new ideas and cover any contingency. The local authority took a dim view of this. Council money was supposed to be spent on local needs not sit in a bank account. The possibility of "clawing back" unspent money was mentioned.

A week later a manager from a potential corporate sponsor visited to assess a proposal the project had made. The manager concluded the review by drawing attention to the lack of any forward financial strategy and that a "well managed organisation should be building up a significant reserve fund for longer term investment".

This case raises three issues:

❶ The need to educate some funders and purchasers for the need for sensible financial management practice.

❷ The importance of managing the relationship with funders. City corporations spend heavily on "investor relations" - a form of internal marketing to stake holders. Could a marketing strategy avoid such frustrations?

❸ A business plan should set out and make the case for a sound financial policy. If an organisation has developed reasonable reserves it needs to explain the reasons for them in a positive and not defensive way in the plan.

MOVING TO A COST CENTRED BUDGET

THE COMMUNITY HEALTH PROJECT

The project is a voluntary run health education project with eight main activities

Education & training:	Courses for teachers, health workers on health matters.
"Good Health" week:	An annual health promotion week.
A rural project:	Community health work with isolated communities.
Resource Centre:	A centre producing and disseminating teaching and resource materials
HIV/AIDS project:	An awareness campaign on HIV/AIDS issues.
Youth project:	Specific health work with 16-22 year olds.
Public Enquiries work:	Enquiry point for a wide range of public calls.
Student Supervision:	Placements for students.

ITS CURRENT BUDGET

INCOME		EXPENDITURE	
Health Authority Contract for public information work	115000	Salaries	124000
Trust grant for rural work	20000	Administration	16000
Government grant for HIV/AIDS work	14000	Resource materials	4000
Income from courses	16000	Minibus	3000
Income from sale/hire of resources	3000	Good Health week	7000
Student placement supervision fees	4000	Telephones	8000
Local council grant for Good Health week	10000	Building costs	20000
TOTAL	**182000**	TOTAL	**182000**

ITS CURRENT STAFF COSTS

Manager	28000	Field Officer	22000
Education Officer	23000	Resources Officer	19000
Information Officer	22000	Clerk(part time)	10000
		TOTAL	**124000**

THE NEED FOR CHANGE

The budget had existed in this format for a number years.

However, four reasons prompted the project's treasurer to recommend moving to a cost centred budget:

◆ The budget did not show the cost of individual activities.
◆ Funders and purchasers wanted to become more "project" based.
◆ There was an urgent need to properly cost and price contracts.
◆ The difficulty of raising money for core running costs.

AGREEING COST CENTRES

The manager and treasurer reviewed the project's work and identified six cost centres. In future all of the project's expenditure would be allocated to one of the six centres:

◆ Education (inc. students)   ◆ Resource Centre (includes Public enquiries)
◆ Good Health Week   ◆ Young People
◆ HIV/AIDS   ◆ Rural Work

MOVING TO A COST CENTRED BUDGET

The first task was to review the original budget's non salary expenditure items and allocate them to each cost centre. The project's building costs were allocated on a fixed percentage basis (based on a rough estimate of how much space each activity took up). The £7000 in the original budget for the Good Health week obviously could be allocated as a direct cost to the Health week cost centre. A quick review of past purchases from the materials budget indicated how it could be allocated between the six centres. The minibus costs were also shared out on the basis of approximate past usage. Some items, such as the admin and telephone budgets proved difficult to allocate as they were mainly shared items. However, it was agreed that a quarter of the phone bill (£2000) and an eighth of the admin budget (£2000) could be allocated as a direct cost to the resource centre's public information work.

BUDGET	Admin	Materials	Minibus	Health Week	Telephones	Building Costs	Total allocation
	16000	4000	3000	7000	8000	20000	
COST CENTRE							
Education		1000				4000	5000
Health Week		200	200	7000		2000	9400
HIV/AIDS		500				3000	3500
Res. Centre	2000	2000			2000	5000	11000
Young people		100	500			3000	3600
Rural Work		200	2000			3000	5200
Not allocated	14000	0	300	0	6000	0	20300

The next stage was for each staff member to review their work and allocate it in broad percentage terms to the six cost centres. The manager and team secretary recognised that a proportion of their work could not be directly allocated to one of the six centres as it was time spent on project wide administration, management and development. This time would be part of the indirect costs of the project. The percentage allocation (and cash equivalent) are shown.

COST CENTRE	Manager	Ed. Officer	Info Officer	Field Officer	Res. Officer	Clerk	Total allocation
Education	20% i.e. 5600	70 i.e. 16100	10% i.e. 2200			10% i.e. 1000	24900
Health Week	10% i.e. 2800	10% i.e. 2300		10% i.e. 2200	20% i.e. 3800		11100
HIV/AIDS	10% i.e. 2800		20% i.e. 4400	20% i.e. 4400	10% i.e. 1900		13500
Res. Centre	10% i.e. 2800	10% i.e. 2300	60% i.e. 13200		60% i.e. 11400	20% i.e. 2000	31700
Young people	5% i.e. 1400		10% i.e. 2200	20% i.e. 4400	10% i.e. 1900		9900
Rural work	5% i.e. 1400	10% i.e. 2300		50% i.e. 11000			14700
Not allocated indirect cost	40% i.e. 11200				70% i.e. 7000		18200
Total	28000	23000	22000	22000	19000	10000	

MOVING TO A COST CENTRED BUDGET

At this stage only the direct costs have been allocated

COST CENTRE	Direct non staff costs	Direct staff costs	TOTAL DIRECT COSTS
Education	5000	24900	**29900**
Health Week	9400	11100	**20500**
HIV/AIDS	3500	13500	**17000**
Resource Centre	11000	31700	**42700**
Young People	3600	9900	**13500**
Rural work	5200	14700	**19900**
Total	37700	105800	

Total direct costs **143500**

Still to be allocated (Indirect costs):

Non staff costs:	20300	**Staff costs:**	18200

Total indirect costs **38500**

The remaining £38500 made up of the £18200 from the salaries budget and £20300 from the non salaries budget still needed to be allocated. The £38500 represents the project's indirect costs. It was shared between the six centres on a percentage formula:

COST CENTRE	% share	Indirect	Direct cost	TOTAL COST CENTRE
Education	20%.	7700	29900	**37600**
Health Week	10%.	3850	20500	**24350**
HIV/AIDS	15%.	5775	17000	**22775**
Resource Centre	25%.	9625	42700	**52325**
Young People	15%.	5775	13500	**19275**
Rural Work	15%.	5775	19900	**25675**
Total		38500	143500	

Total cost **182000**

DRAWING UP A CASH FLOW PROJECTION

A community arts organisation worked out its likely cash flow projection as follows:

opening cash balance:		500	21130	14920	14740	7640	1190	-980	14300	11180	5160	3690	1420

INCOME	12 mths	April	May	June	July	Aug	Sept	Oct	Nov	Dec	Jan	Feb	March
Council grant	30000	15000						15000					
Arts Board	25000	10000						10000			5000		
Sponsorship	14000			6000					4000			4000	
Fee Income	12000	2000					5000			1000			4000
Building hire	9000	900	700	500	300	100	300	500	1000	1700	1400	800	800
Rent income	6000	500	500	500	500	500	500	500	500	500	500	500	500
Donations/Misc	4000	400	350	350	250	250	300	400	350	350	300	350	350
TOTAL INCOME	100000												
monthly income:		28800	1550	7350	1050	850	6100	26400	5850	3550	7200	5650	5650

EXPENDITURE													
Salaries	42500	3220	3260	3330	3500	3500	3670	3670	3670	3670	3670	3670	3670
Building cost	13000	1100	1000	1200	1000	1000	1000	1000	1600	1100	1000	1000	1000
Admin	18750	2000	1600	1500	1500	1400	1500	1500	1600	1600	1550	2000	1000
Phones	3000	750			750			750			750		
Festival	7000			600	200	500	1200	3000	700	800	100	100	
Projects	7750	700	1300	500	800	300	500	500	500	800	1000	350	500
Equipment	8000	400	600	400	400	600	400	700	900	1600	600	800	600
TOTAL EXP.	100000												
monthly expenditure:		8170	7760	7530	8150	7300	8270	11120	8970	9570	8670	7920	6770
closing cash balance		21130	14920	14740	7640	1190	-980	14300	11180	5160	3690	1420	300

The closing cash balance is:
The opening balance PLUS monthly income LESS monthly expenditure

The opening balance for the next month is:
The closing balance for the previous month

A FINANCIAL HEALTH CHECK

This exercise aims to help the planning process by focusing on three issues:

◆ The recent and current financial management and performance of the organisation.

◆ The importance of developing a coherent financial policy for the organisation.

◆ The need to think about finance in a strategic way and not simply a bureaucratic way.

Think about the past few years and future possibilities and answer the following questions:

① FINANCIAL HISTORY

How effective has the organisation been at costing projects? Have budgets usually been accurate or have certain costs been ignored or badly estimated?

- -

- -

- -

- -

- -

- -

What has been the pattern of cash flow in the organisation? Have there been any regular peaks and troughs?

- -

- -

- -

- -

- -

- -

How have costs been allocated in the organisation? Have the indirect costs (i.e. management charges, administrative overheads) **been properly recognised and reasonably shared out?**

- -

- -

- -

- -

- -

- -

A FINANCIAL HEALTH CHECK

What has the balance sheet looked like? What has been the liquidity ratio i.e. how much cash (current assets) **has been available to pay off current liabilities?**

② FINANCIAL MANAGEMENT SYSTEMS

Has there usually been adequate systems of financial control within the organisation?

Do budget holders receive information which is up to date, relevant and accurately monitors planned income and expenditure against actual performance.

A FINANCIAL HEALTH CHECK

Does the organisation's financial system give accurate information on what specific services and projects cost (including their contribution to the organisation's indirect costs)**?**

- -
- -
- -
- -
- -
- -
- -

Are any particular costs volatile or highly variable? How will this effect the business plan? Can they be controlled better?

- -
- -
- -
- -
- -
- -
- -
- -

Are there sufficient financial skills within the organisation to:

☐ Control income and expenditure   ☐ Accurately cost projects   ☐ Develop & project financial plans

Do you anticipate any modifications to your budgeting or accounting systems? What improvements are needed

- -
- -
- -
- -
- -
- -
- -

A FINANCIAL HEALTH CHECK

➌ FINANCIAL POLICY

Is sufficient income set aside for reserves and contingency?

What proportion of the organisation's turnover would be a reasonable amount to carry as a reserve or contingency fund?

Is sufficient income set aside to cover depreciation and for replacement costs?

Are the full costs of operating services and projects known?

What are your minimum operating costs per month?

Is the balance between central charges and direct project costs a fair one?

A FINANCIAL HEALTH CHECK

④ FINANCIAL PROJECTIONS

Over the next two years which income sources do you predict will decline?

- -

Over the next two years which income sources do you predict will increase?

- -

- -

⑤ FLEXIBILITY OF YOUR INCOME?

What proportion of your income is "earmarked" or committed for a particular expenditure i.e. its use is restricted**?**

- -

- -

What proportion of your income is dedicated from one year to another (for, example salaries for permanent staff, contractual obligations to suppliers)**?**

- -

- -

Does current spending accurately reflect current priorities?

- -

What direct product costs could be reduced?

- -

What indirect organisational overheads could be reduced?

- -

- -

A FINANCIAL HEALTH CHECK

⑥ FINANCIAL STRATEGIES

Can you anticipate any significant changes in your organisational cost base over the next few years?

Is there a coherent policy behind the charges that you make for your services to statutory purchasers, funders and consumers?

What sort of pricing strategy do you currently use?

How does this compare to other organisations doing similar work?

How might this change?

TEN COSTS OFTEN IGNORED

The following ten costs are ones which are often under estimated or simply ignored.

① Start up costs

One off costs involved with launching or establishing a project. Staff recruitment costs, moving in costs, building adaptions and launch publicity costs are often underestimated or create an early cash flow problem.

② Slow start costs

Sometimes services start more slowly than anticipated. Organisations that sell their services or receive unit or spot contracts can experience below target performance at what can often be an expensive time due to extra costs involved in the service's start up.

③ Marketing costs

Publicity costs, communication and image-building costs are often ignored leading to poor or amateurish public relations that can cause credibility problems.

④ Costs of democracy and governance

Often projects and services have advisory panels and sub-committees to guide their work. The cost of establishing such bodies, training their members and servicing them needs to be included.

⑤ Research and development costs

Costs involved in user consultation, needs identification and service evaluation are often expensive and should be built into service budgets and plans to demonstrate good management practice.

⑥ Cash flow costs

Many organisations operate to very tight cash flow plans. A delayed payment from a funder or unanticipated expense can easily knock a budget off course. Anticipating cash flow problems and making necessary arrangements to survive a cash shortage can lead to extra costs.

⑦ Management and administrative costs

An extra project will usually demand extra management and administrative time and space from the main organisation. There is a danger of simply adding projects and activities on until the systems break down. Extra admin time, payroll costs, computer usage and management time all need to be calculated. Volunteer management is another related cost.

⑧ Replacement and repair costs

Capital items will usually need to be replaced at some stage. Items such as computers, office equipment and other resources will need replacing at some stage. Buildings will need decoration on a regular basis. Many organisations have a replacement fund which accumulates cash for such costs. Is the contribution to the replacement fund sufficient?

⑨ Contingency costs

Staff maternity leave, sickness cover, legal costs and emergency repairs are all examples of contingency costs. Some organisations now hold a central contingency fund to which all projects contribute. Some contingency costs can be met by insurance cover.

⑩ Close down costs

There will often be costs involved in closing down a fixed term project that need to be built in. These could include evaluation costs, accounting charges, repairs and replacement costs of loaned equipment and buildings and staff costs.

TEN COSTS OFTEN IGNORED

How well does your organisation cost it's services?

Over the past few years have any of the ten costs been regularly overlooked or underestimated?

Are there any other costs that have been regularly overlooked or underestimated?

What can your organisation realistically do to improve how it costs it's services and projects?

PREDICTING TRENDS IN CURRENT INCOME

In column A, list all your current sources of income. In column B, note the proportion of your income this particular source currently represents. Also note any other relevant details for example, if the income is scheduled to end. In column C, describe what you currently know or predict is likely to happen to this income source (eg. will it get bigger or smaller or will the availability of it change?). In column D, note any action that you need to take to secure or better manage this income source.

A INCOME	B CURRENT POSITION	C PREDICTION OF TRENDS	D ACTION NEEDED

Chapter ⑥

SETTING THE STRATEGIC DIRECTION

After clarifying what the organisation is for, taking stock of its development to date and obtaining a clearer financial picture, the planning process can now move onto setting a strategic direction.

Different definitions of strategy exist. In most definitions of organisational strategy the following elements are present:

◆ Making decisions about priorities.

◆ Linking current activities to future plans.

◆ Setting a direction or route for the organisation.

◆ Obtaining resources for the new direction.

◆ Managing change and setting objectives.

Most organisations (public, private or voluntary) were designed to allow vertical systems of command and control. People at the top of the organisation make important decisions and plans that are transmitted down the organisation by managers and supervisors to the people who should then carry them out.

SENIOR MANAGERS

MANAGERS

STAFF

TRADITIONAL STRUCTURE

In many organisations these levels do not link together at all well. Policy makers (senior managers and committee members) churn out policy papers, develop plans and demand change. People working at the operations level feel frustrated that new initiatives from the top and "change for change's sake" gets in the way of the real work of the organisation. Any sense of strategy that links policy to the day to day work is missing.

Other criticisms of this structure are that it mitigates against team work, slows down communication (as the structure gets bigger) and cuts off senior managers from seeing the impact of their work. Effective business planning and strategic management requires good internal communication, good feedback and an ability to think about the whole of the organisation and not just specific departments.

○ ○ ○ ○ ○ ○ ○

A CREDIBLE ASSUMPTION?

The chief officers and leading councillors of a local authority adopted a survival strategy. They were faced with a recently elected government determined to "roll back the state", cut capital and revenue spending and restrict local government powers. Short term creative accounting schemes, damage limitation and "hoping for a government more in line with our way of thinking" was the order of the day in 1979. "Getting by until the next election" was the implicit strategic direction.

After fourteen years (and three general elections), is the strategic assumption that "in a few years time a change of government will make everything better" a sensible one? Years of crisis management, organisational turmoil and lack of clear direction has left an organisation feeling demoralised and drifting. What might have been a reasonable assumption in 1979 is today found lacking. The failure to explore other scenarios and the unwillingness to question or challenge previous assumptions have taken their toll of political, managerial and organisational confidence.

Often strategic management is about deciding what not to do as much as what to do. One charity Director summed up this problem by referring to priorities. "My organisation is brilliant at making priorities. We have hundreds, and they are all equally important. Every time I talk to my board or staff about the need to make priorities, I end up getting a few more."

This chapter will look at four issues:

❶ Establishing the assumptions behind the plan.

❷ Identification of the organisation's limits.

❸ Identifying strategic choices.

❹ Agreeing and setting a strategic direction

ESTABLISHING THE ASSUMPTIONS BEHIND THE PLAN

Any planning process involves making some assumptions upon which planning can be based. Some commercial planners develop complex future based scenarios to test out future possibilities. Other people rely on intelligent and informed guesswork. A business plan should set out the central assumptions behind it as readers of it might wish to know the assumptions upon which the rest of the plan is made.

One approach is to list key assumptions under a series of headings:

ASSUMPTIONS ~ Examples of assumptions made

Assumptions need to be credible, discussed openly and periodically checked. The danger of operating with an assumption that no longer applies is commonplace.

Demand and needs	*"That referrals will stay at the same rate over the next two years"*
	"That demand for respite care will continue to rise".
External developments	*"That the local authorities will increasingly move towards spot or user based contracts".*

*"That other agencies who
work in this field will continue to
charge a similar fee to ours".*

**Internal
developments**

*"That we will still be able to recruit
support and retain a volunteer
team at its current level".*

*"That staff turnover will remain at
its current level"*

Financial

*"That for the next two years
increases in fee rates will
meet inflation and pay awards"*

*"That our fund raising income
will rise by 5% each year for the
next three years".*

IDENTIFICATION OF THE ORGANISATION'S LIMITS

All organisations have limits. Discussion of organisational
strategy without reference to the organisation's limits is
pointless day dreaming. Different sorts of limits exist. Some
are fixed and some are more negotiable.

Possible limits include:

Physical

*"Our current office could only cope
with one more member of staff".*

**Legal &
constitutional**

*"Moving into this area of work could
take us beyond our legal powers as a
charity".*

**Level of
manageable risk**

*"To run this number of innovative
and pioneering projects would be
unacceptable to our trustees".*

Human

*"Our current staff team are not
skilled in this area of work".*

Resource

*"To develop in such a way would
stretch our management and
communication systems".*

Financial

*"To continue with this kind of
funding will seriously harm our cash flow".*

A LIMIT ON STRATEGY

The "honeymoon period" in Kerry's new job as development manager for a charity for people with learning difficulties did not last long. She had been employed to research, design and set up new projects and initiatives. The charity desperately needed to improve its services and develop a commitment to user involvement. In her first few months, she developed proposals for three small projects. At first the reaction of her colleagues was very supportive.

Every six months managers met together for a planning day. The bulk of Kerry's first meeting was given over to consideration of her proposals. None of the managers present disagreed in principle with the proposals. However, each proposal was subject to detailed examination of the potential risk, the financial implications and the other costs. Kerry agreed to produce further reports and feasibility studies.

Three months after the strategy day, all of the projects were starting to "slide off the drawing board". However much extra information she produced, the projects were still being deferred.

Kerry fully understood that all new proposals needed rigorous review. However, she felt frustrated that many of the charity's current services were poor or in decline, but were never subject to any kind of review at all. Some were even at odds with the charity's recent statement of values and vision. Once projects had been established and up and running they carried on being allocated resources every year regardless. It was as if strategic management only applied to the consideration of new things and not to looking at current activities.

Usually the most obvious limits are the resource or financial ones. However, it is interesting to look at how an organisation's traditions, practices and long term commitments can also be a limiting factor.

Three questions are useful in reviewing the limiting factors:

❶ How fixed is each limiting factor?

❷ What creates the limiting factor?

❸ What would we have to do to change it?

A useful exercise is to consider how the organisation would be different if it were to be created today. What would the organisation look like? What services would be provided? What would be the relationship to service users? It is interesting that many limiting factors are the direct product of the organisation's history. Some organisations have adopted a technique called zero base budgeting. Managers rebuild the budget for each activity as if they were starting it again. The case for expenditure and staff time has to be justified against the organisation's strategy. It is interesting as a result of this exercise how many limiting factors are challenged as resources previously committed are redirected to other priorities.

IDENTIFYING STRATEGIC CHOICES

All organisations have choices available to them. Doing nothing is one choice. Identifying choices and options for the future should be a participatory process that involves all individuals.

A useful approach is to start by posing options for the future. Possible options might include:

◆ Should we grow, stay the same or get smaller?

◆ What aspects of our work should we do more of or less of?

◆ What geographic areas should we do more in or less in?

- What style of work should we do more of or less of?

- Which client groups should we target?

- Should we become more specialist or more generalist?

- What alliances or relationships with others should we develop?

At this stage it is useful to bring into the discussion the users perspective and the organisation mission. The focus of the direction needs to be on what the outside world needs and not just what feels comfortable for people in the organisation.

The list of options probably will be more than the organisation can deal with, so some sort of clear criteria is needed to evaluate possible choice. One agency worked through the following five points in relation to each option that emerged:

- What is (or should be) distinctive about us as an organisation? Does this strategic option fit with our core mission and values?

- What are we effective at? What works? What do we do consistently well?

- Is our expertise best suited to this option?

- What are our priorities? What needs are most important to meet? Does this option fit with our priorities?

- Will this option be financially viable or if not is it important enough to subsidise it? Will we be able to deliver?

Each option was applied to the above criteria and graded accordingly. A number were quickly rejected, others were combined together and five were picked as the main driving force of the organisation.

AGREEING AND SETTING A STRATEGIC DIRECTION

Agreeing a strategic direction and aims involves constant reference back to the limiting factors and the overall mission. The process involves a continual movement between generating options, making priorities and working within the limiting factors.

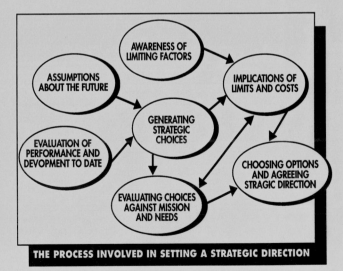

THE PROCESS INVOLVED IN SETTING A STRATEGIC DIRECTION

MOVING FROM MISSION THROUGH STRATEGY TO OBJECTIVES

The Eastside business advice agency, was set up to help inner city residents explore the possibility of becoming self employed and creating small businesses. It is strongly committed to equal opportunities and full access to its services.

The agency's mission is: *"To provide high quality advice, training and support to emerging or newly created small businesses. The agency exists to support a viable and sustainable local economy. In carrying out this mission it will ensure that the highest standards of quality assurance and equal opportunities apply throughout."*

Specific Aims

The agency agreed four strategic aims to guide all of its work over the next two years:

◆ To continue to provide affordable and effective advice, counselling and information services to new or potential businesses.

◆ To provide a high quality training programme for business owners in three areas: management skills, marketing and quality assurance.

◆ To support cooperation between new businesses, encourage the marketing of inner city businesses and identify new business opportunities.

◆ To investigate and pilot ways of supporting businesses facing insolvency.

Specific Objectives

For aim 3, "To support cooperation between new businesses, encourage the marketing of inner city businesses and identify new business opportunities." there are six objectives:

◆ To encourage three inner city business networks through monthly breakfast seminars and quarterly business forums. The forums should aim to attract 150 participants in total (100 hours).

◆ To organise four self financing business advertisement campaigns promoting local business (30 hours).

◆ To create a woman's business forum that will have a minimum of 20 participants and be able to be self managing (60 hours, to be implemented by February).

◆ To organise an inner city business exhibition target attendance 400 people (300 hours, planned date in October, budget: £12,000).

◆ To have developed and implemented a strategy to raise funds for a food purchasing and distribution cooperative (75 hours, first report to January management committee).

◆ To participate in the management committee of the electronic village steering group (45 hours).

The objectives were produced by the relevant team member. They estimated how much time they would spend on each item as an indicator of priorities. The objectives became the work plan for each staff member.

At each stage the language of the plan changes. The mission statement will be hard to measure and act on. It is a statement of intent, not of specific action. The strategic aims need to indicate the clear direction and priority of the organisation for its immediate future. The objectives should be task centred and provide a measurable work plan for the organisation.

Many business plans use a format of a plan that cascades through different levels:

The mission — The purpose and values statement.

Strategic aims — A limited number of priorities. A route for the organisation to follow

Objectives — Costed, detailed and timed action plans for each strategic aim.

Experience in several organisations is that anything more than six to seven strategic aims leads to a plan (and an organisation) that is fragmented, confused and pulling in different directions.

Strategic aims need to:

◆ Indicate a clear direction.

◆ Be focused on intended outcomes.

◆ Be integrated with other aims.

◆ Be realistic and attainable.

Determining a future strategy often involves difficult decisions. Turning down someone's favourite project, deciding to withdraw from an area of work or shifting resources from one area to another will usually involve anxiety and conflict. As much attention will have to be paid to what the organisation is not going to do as to what it is.

Once the strategic aims have been agreed, objectives need to be established for each area. A well used mnemonic for writing objectives is **SMART.**

There is a danger that senior managers will write too much of the plan. Clearly trustees and managers have the responsibility for the mission and agreeing the strategic aims, but, if they involve themselves in the detail of the operational objectives then the plan will never properly become the property of the organisation.

S SPECIFIC
M MEASURABLE
A ATTAINABLE
R REALISTIC
T TIMED

One agency adopted a four stage approach to agreeing its strategy. First a joint staff and management committee meeting agreed a mission statement. After considerable discussion the management committee agreed five aims. Each aim was then delegated to an appropriate staff group who reviewed their activities and worked out a detailed work plan within the boundary set by the core aims. The management committee then agreed all of the work objectives.

HOW CLEAR IS THE DIRECTION?

This exercise is useful to attempt after the main strategic aims of the organisation have been agreed. If the answers are uncertain or vague, then it may mean that the direction agreed is not decisive enough.

If the strategic aims are successfully implemented.....
What will be different about the organisation?

Will the organisation be:

Bigger or smaller?

Doing more things (or fewer things)?

The same users (or different ones)?

Generalist (or more targeted)?

Working in the same ways (or different ways)?

Alterations and changes your organisation anticipate:

What will be the key differences if this strategy is implemented?

_____

_____

_____

Try to describe the significant changes of the new direction as if you were writing a newspaper headline.

_____

_____

_____

What will still be the same?

_____

_____

What will the organisation do more and less of?

More of

_____

_____

_____

Less of

_____

_____

_____

WHAT'S THE LIMIT?

Think about your organisation. What are the limiting factors to its growth and development?

LIMITING FACTOR	HOW FIXED IS IT?	STRATEGIES TO OVERCOME IT?

WHEN DID YOU LAST HAVE A NEW IDEA?

Many voluntary organisations pride themselves on being innovative. They see themselves as being dynamic and challenging. What is the reality?

One worker in a national organisation described her organisation's approach to new ideas as:

"If someone has an idea that they want to push for they have to be prepared to run an obstacle course of working groups, consultation meetings and discussion papers. It will take months. Any plan that emerges, (and quite a few don't) will have had any inventive or creative element drained out of it".

Managing new ideas and creating innovation tests many organisations. The following exercise aims to help you to evaluate the capacity of your organisation to be innovative and ensure that the plan does have a creative element.

List any new or dynamic ideas or initiatives that have got off the drawing board in your organisation in the past two years:

- -

- -

- -

- -

- -

What are the factors that encourage innovation in the organisation?

- -

- -

- -

- -

What are the factors that discourage innovation in the organisation?

- -

- -

- -

- -

What does the organisation do to encourage new ideas? (possible examples could include: having a research and development budget, evaluating current services, encouraging project teams etc.)

- -

- -

- -

- -

- -

WHEN DID YOU LAST HAVE A NEW IDEA?

How could this be improved?

What happens when new ideas or innovative projects go wrong?

What is the balance of the plan between ongoing work and new work in the plan?

How can new ideas, creative strategies and innovative work be encouraged in the planning process?

Chapter 7

ESTABLISHING CREDIBILTY

A business plan needs to make the case for an organisation. It needs to establish confidence in the minds of potential backers that the organisation is competent enough to successfully manage the plan. A manager of a trust that requires business plans as part of its application process commented, "The idea behind the plan may well be brilliant. But, we need to know that it has the people and systems in place to implement it. We look to the business plan to convince us that the organisation has a track record and that the key personnel involved are experienced in similar activities."

The business plan can demonstrate this in four ways:

❶ Growing evidence that the organisation has a history of sound practice and good management.

❷ Establishing that the organisation has in place systems and structures which are appropriate to the scale and demands of the plan.

❸ Showing that the organisation has within it a core of personnel with sufficient skills to implement the plan.

❹ Proving that, in the case of new initiatives, sufficient feasibility work on the plan has been carried out.

Many voluntary organisations seem reluctant or unwilling to positively record or market their own expertise, skills and competence. The process of collecting this information can have some very useful side effects. It can put them in a much stronger position with funders and purchasers, and it can also increase the organisation's own confidence in itself. For smaller organisations or newer projects the plan might need to show that there are sufficient support systems around it to help it.

COLLECTING EVIDENCE

The following six points are possible sources of evidence that an organisation has a good track record:

❶ **Financial records**
Previous accounts and audits could show that the organisation has properly managed its financial affairs in the past.

② External evaluations

Recorded evaluation studies could indicate strengths of the organisation.

③ Feedback from users

Client reaction, client follow up and repeat work could indicate that the organisation is capable of providing a service that people want.

④ Third party references

Sponsorship from "eminent" persons could establish credibility. A health group used backing from medical consultants in its business plan to establish credibility with health purchasers.

⑤ Client list

A list of current or past organisational clients or partners could indicate credibility particularly if client organisations agreed to act as referees.

⑥ Evidence of successful work

Press cuttings, case studies and case follow ups might create a positive feel about the organisation.

○ ○ ○ ○ ○ ○ ○ ○ ○

PROVING CREDIBILITY

The Family in Crisis charity was a new group set up by parents and some professionals to provide counselling, support and help to families in times of turmoil and stress. Initially the group worked with a network of volunteers coordinated by a worker paid for by a trust. However, changes in community care prompted the committee to approach the Health Authority to discuss how they might work together and the possibilities of financial support.

The first discussion with the Health Authority was positive. The charity's services fitted in extremely well with several elements of the community care plan and with current priorities. The authority asked for a business plan so that they could consider it further.

The draft business plan followed a format set out in a high street bank's new business guide. The section asking them to "list the relevant experience of key personnel" was initially hard. The Heath Authority officer had commented that it was of concern to them that all "potential providers were professional". At first this was seen by the committee as a weakness as they were "only volunteers". Surely the criteria favoured businesses or statutory organisations and put a small voluntary organisation at a disadvantage.

The committee carried out a mapping exercise to list the various skills they had. Amongst the committee's membership were a finance manager in a private company, a retired headteacher, a legal executive and a woman who had set up and ran a successful small business. The group had within it significant management expertise, but, perhaps as important, was their combined local knowledge, contacts and personal experience of living with and surviving family crisis.

The charity also had around it a network of people who had during different stages of the charity's history provided help and support. They included two doctors, an assistant director of social services and a psychotherapist. These individuals agreed to form an advisory panel to the charity, separate from the management structure, that would advise the management committee and ensure a quality service.

Despite initial doubts, it was now clear that for the size of the organisation the charity had within or around it considerable skills and experience.

DEMONSTRATING ORGANISATIONAL COMPETENCE

A business plan needs to show that the organisation has in place the systems and processes necessary to properly manage the plan. The following five areas might provide some evidence:

❶ Evidence of good organisational practice

The existence of an equal opportunities policy, complaints procedure, staff development policies and other statements might show that, on paper at least, the organisation is clear about how it should work.

❷ A quality assurance policy

Quality assurance is about three things; finding out from

users what is important about how the service operates, establishing minimum quality standards that indicate what can be expected from a service and ensuring that the organisation consistently meets the standards. A quality assurance policy should set out key standards and indicate how they will be monitored and improved.

❸ An external award

In some industries the award of the British quality standard, BS5750, is an almost mandatory requirement. Some contracts are only be awarded to companies with BS5750 accreditation. All BS5750 indicates is that the management practices used to manage a system are rigorous and comprehensive enough to satisfy an external audit. It does not comment on the benefit to users of the service being provided or the relevance of the standards set. Another external standard is Investors In People, IPP, which is awarded after an external review of an organisation's staff training and development policies.

❹ Membership of a national organisation

Many smaller organisations or projects could point to their membership of a national organisation as evidence of having back up services such as training, specialist advice and information. The national organisation might also provide some quality assurance function.

❺ Audits and inspections

Evidence of successful external inspections (for example Registered Homes Act) could also be used to show that the organisation is well managed.

COMPETENCE OF KEY PEOPLE

Some business plans include the outline curriculum vitae of all the management team members. This may be going into too much detail, but the following information might help convince backers that the organisation has within it sufficient skilled people:

◆ Background details and experience of key staff.

◆ Background details and experience of management committee and trustees.

◆ Names of external advisers, accountants, solicitors and specialist consultants.

◆ Relevant qualified staff.

◆ Staff development policies.

PROVING THAT A NEW PROJECT IS FEASIBLE

Many small businesses (and possibly some voluntary projects) fail because the individuals who start them up are so full of passion for their project that it gets in the way of any genuine feasibility study. The commitment to the vision and dream becomes so important that questions such as will it work and who will pay for it are seen as negative and diversionary. For a new project the business plan needs to set out:

◆ How the need for it has been identified.

◆ What the need is.

◆ What support there is for the project.

◆ How the proposed project will meet the need.

◆ What will be the start up costs.

◆ How the project will be researched and tested.

Evidence should be included to show that possible pitfalls and alternatives have been explored. A useful exercise is to try to predict all of the potential questions and challenges there will be to the project and then assemble evidence to answer them. It is also useful in discussing a project's feasibility to identify in the business plan potential risks involved in the project and suggest how that risk can best be managed. It is better to acknowledge a risk first and deal with it than to let someone else identify it as an undisclosed weakness.

PROVING YOUR TRACK RECORD

A business plan should show that the organisation is capable of achieving its plan. It will need to show evidence that the organisation or the key people within it have the competence and experience to successfully manage the plan.

What evidence do you have of the following elements:

Sound financial management?

_____

_____

A consistent quality of service?

_____

_____

Effective response to needs?

_____

_____

Good management practice?

_____

_____

What other strengths or organisational assets need highlighting in the plan?

_____

_____

_____

_____

_____

_____

_____

_____

_____

_____

_____

PRESENTING THE BUSINESS PLAN

Putting the business plan on paper is an important task. The document needs to be concise, present the plans for the organisation and convince people that the organisation is credible. There is some debate as to whether organisations should produce a single document for all audiences or whether there should be different documents for different uses.

A business plan needs to give an honest appraisal of an organisation's development to date. It should note weaknesses and setbacks, as well as strengths and achievements. Some of the most effective plans are the ones that give a full picture of an organisation, and also clearly indicate what action management will be taking to improve performance where it has been lacking.

There is sometimes a problem with releasing a business plan that could be of value to a "competitor". A manager of a training centre experienced this problem when required to produce a business plan for a tender to manage a government training programme. She explained that, "Our business plan contained details of how we cost our work, staffing levels and management arrangements. This information represented the product of years of work on trying to get the service right. We have always worked in a very open way, but, I would be unhappy if some of the agencies we now compete with had sight of it. We did submit it, but, on the condition that it's circulation was restricted."

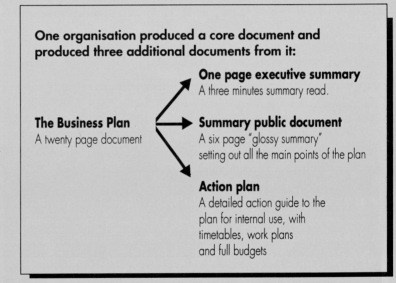

One organisation produced a core document and produced three additional documents from it:

The Business Plan
A twenty page document

One page executive summary
A three minutes summary read.

Summary public document
A six page "glossy summary" setting out all the main points of the plan

Action plan
A detailed action guide to the plan for internal use, with timetables, work plans and full budgets

The business plan itself followed a format similar to the one described in this book. It was made available to funders and purchasers, who could request any further information. The one page executive summary was attached to the business plan as a covering document and also used in presentations about the organisation. It was particularly useful for dealing with politicians who had little time to read the full document and only really needed to know the overall direction. The summary document was a freely available publication circulated to the public. The action plan was described by one staff member as a "management bible" and regularly used by staff working to the plan.

The executive summary is particularly important. It is easy to get lost in the detail of the plan itself. It is important to remember that many potential backers use the summary, or in its absence a two minute glance through the full document, to get " a feel of the plan" . This first impression can often greatly influence future considerations. The executive summary should highlight the main features of the organisation, set out its direction and make clear what is expected from others.

Careful thought needs to be given to the style and format of the business plan itself. It is useful to list the main messages (no more than five) that you want the plan to convey and organise the rest of the information and evidence around them. Some business plans suffer from being written by people who are so close to the organisation that they can not see it as an outsider would. Obvious pieces of information are forgotten, jargon is used and assumptions made. It is worthwhile to get someone distant from the organisation to read it through or to edit it.

Six points are worth remembering:

❶ The document should be no longer than thirty pages. After that it is probable that there will be so much detail that the main direction will be lost.

❷ Do not assume that people understand what the organisation does or what the needs of its users are. This can even apply to people who have been donating income for years.

❸ Use summaries and action points to create a feeling of direction and purpose.

❹ Think carefully about how to present financial information. Make sure that the assumptions behind future forecasts are stated.

❺ Use graphs and charts to explain information, but, check that their meaning is not distorted by them.

❻ Keep the style and language of the document active and task centred. It should be clear and specific not vague and ambiguous.

A one page executive Summary

EASTSIDE BUSINESS AGENCY

The Agency is a registered charity and established as a company limited by guarantee. Established in 1987 it operates in the east side of the city, an area of declining employment, high adult unemployment and social deprivation. The Agency's mission is,

"To provide high quality advice, training and support to emerging or newly created small businesses. The Agency exists to support a viable and sustainable local economy. In carrying out this mission it will ensure that the highest standards of quality assurance and equal opportunities apply throughout."

The Agency's seven strong staff team provide initial advice for those considering self employment, practical help with business start ups, training and consultancy, joint marketing and continued contact with new businesses in their first three years of operation. We deal with an average of forty five new or potential new businesses at any one time. A recent evaluation shows that the Agency has helped to create 126 new businesses in Eastside employing nearly 300 people. 39% of our clients are from the Black and Asian communities.

The Agency has developed successful partnerships and funding arrangements with the City Council, the Training and Enterprise Council and the City Challenge. One of the high points of last year was the award of the Investors in People standard as a recognition of our commitment to staff development.

This two year business plan has two central themes. The consolidation of the Agency's work and the development of new services to help established businesses survive the difficult trading climate.

The plan puts forward four strategic aims. The first two will consolidate our existing advice, counselling and information services and continue our popular business training programme. Our third aim is to encourage practical cooperation and joint marketing of existing businesses. Our fourth aim is to pilot new ways of providing assistance to businesses approaching or facing insolvency. This is a new area of work for the Agency and is in response to growing enquiries from our clients.

The plan sets out how this strategy can be achieved with backing at an equivalent level from our current partners, the gradual closure of our grants advisory service and the creation of a new post of marketing support manager.

The organisation is now an established and proven Agency working within the inner city. This plan sets out a two year future for its continued success.

THE STRUCTURE OF A BUSINESS PLAN

SECTION	CONTENT
1 **An "executive summary"**	Brief outline of mission, values and context. It should highlight the proposed direction, key benefits and make the case for the organisation. A one page, three minutes read.
2 **Introduction & mission**	The mission statement in full. Explanation of purpose and duration of the plan.
3 **The organisation's background**	A brief history of the organisation. Its legal status and registered office. Include limited and useful information that would help the reader get a picture of it eg. staff numbers, user profile and areas of operation.
4 **A summary review**	A short review of the organisation to date. Stress strengths, achievements and external recognition to date. Readers may expect to see some honest appraisal of weaknesses. A SWOT analysis is often used to display this information.
5 **Future trends**	An outline of how the organisation sees its future environment developing. Refer to likely needs of users. The plan needs to show that thought has been given to likely external developments.
6 **Strategic direction**	What assumptions underpin the chosen direction. What will be the main push of the organisation's work? What will be its main priorities? What will be different?

THE STRUCTURE OF A BUSINESS PLAN

SECTION   CONTENT

⌐ Strategic aims   Statement of aims for the medium term. The specific objectives
                                 for each aim could be listed or a brief summary of them given.

ℰ Implications   Areas or work that will be dropped or phased out should be
                                 noted. Organisational, legal or any other key
                                 implications should be listed.

ꝗ Financial   How will the plan be funded? Income and
implications   expenditure projections for the first year and estimates for
                                 following years. Listing of financial assumptions behind the
                                 plan. Statement of key financial policy (eg. pricing policy)
                                 and evidence of efficient management (eg. cash flow
                                 forecast).

ⁱᵒTrack record of   Making the case for the organisation. Showing that it has
the organisation   the management competence and experience necessary to
                                 manage the plan. The past experience of the organisation
                                 and its key personnel could be listed. A list of critical success
                                 factors.

ⁱⁱ

Immediate   Timed action for the first steps in the plan.
action plan

PUTTING THE PLAN ON PAPER

This exercise will help to organise your thinking about the plan and structure the organisation of the relevant information. In the box note the information that you need to collect, any decisions that you need to make and summarise your response to the key points.

Section	Key points
"Executive summary"	What are the main points (no more than five) that you want readers to remember about the plan?

_____
_____
_____
_____
_____

Introduction & mission	Can you sum up the organisation's purpose in no more than forty words?

_____
_____
_____
_____
_____
_____
_____
_____
_____
_____
_____

The organisation's background	What background information about the organisation do readers need to know to understand the plan?

_____
_____
_____
_____
_____

PUTTING THE PLAN ON PAPER

Section	Key points
A summary review	Sum up the organisation's record to date. Avoid going into too much detail.
Future trends	Set out the bigger picture. What will the organisation's future environment look like - users profile, trends, needs and opportunities?
Strategic direction	What assumptions are you making about the future? What are the organisation's main priorities for the next period?

PUTTING THE PLAN ON PAPER

Section	Key points
Strategic aims	Statement of core aims for the organisation as a whole - no more than six.
	Specific objectives on how each aim will be implemented.
Implications	To meet this plan what will you have to do differently?
	What changes in how the organisation currently works will have to be managed?

PUTTING THE PLAN ON PAPER

Section	Key points	
Financial implications	How will the plan be funded? Financial projections and estimates. Summary of financial policy.	
Track record of the organisation	Evidence that the organisation is capable of meeting the plan.	
	What are your critical success factors?	
Immediate action plan	Detailed implementation plan for the first steps.	

EVALUATING YOUR PLAN

Does your plan create a clear sense of
purpose or mission that all of the
organisation can work for?

- -

- -

- -

- -

- -

Action Points

- -

Are all of the strategic aims and
detailed objectives in the plan
consistent with the mission?

- -

- -

- -

- -

- -

Action Points

- -

Are you confident that you have
adequately gathered information about
possible external events, trends and
possibilities that will affect your
organisation's future?

- -

- -

- -

- -

- -

Action Points

- -

EVALUATING YOUR PLAN

On a continuum ranging from "bleakly pessimistic" to "wildly optimistic" evaluate the main decisions and aims within the plan?

← ── →

Bleakly pessimistic   **Wildly optimistic**

Do any of these
decisions and
aims cause you
concern?

Action Points

On a continuum ranging from "wild guess" to "guaranteed forecast" evaluate the main forecasts and projections in the plan?

← ── →

Wild guess   **Guaranteed forecast**

Do any of these
forecasts and
projections cause you
concern?

Action Points

On a continuum of "mission impossible" to "will be easy to achieve" evaluate the specific objectives and work commitments set out in the plan.

← ── →

Mission impossible   **Easy to achieve**

Do any of these
specific objectives and
work commitments
cause you concern

Action Points

EVALUATING YOUR PLAN

List the five main messages that you would like readers of the plan to retain:

❶ -

- -

❷ -

- -

❸ -

- -

❹ -

- -

❺ -

- -

How clearly does the plan
convey these points?

- -

- -

- -

- -

How will you know if the
plan has worked? What
feedback and monitoring
systems will you use?

- -

- -

- -

- -

What will be the first steps
after agreeing the plan?
What will be your
immediate action plan?

- -

- -

- -

- -

Chapter 9

MANAGING THE PLAN
• PUTTING IT INTO PRACTICE •

As described in the introduction to this book, several organisations invest time in the planning process, produce a business plan and then file it away. It is forgotten until it has to be worked on again. The plan remains a paper document that gathers dust on the shelf. Three reasons might contribute to this:

1 The plan never really dealt with the realities of the organisation. It is all about how people would like it to be in a perfect world.

2 The process of putting the plan together never engaged people who need to implement it. The managers or external consultants who drove the planning process never created a feeling of ownership throughout the organisation.

3 The plan itself is fine, but managers do not have either the time or the skill to manage the changes involved.

The first two issues are dealt with earlier in this book. This chapter will focus on the processes involved in overcoming the third issue. It deals with five questions:

1 How to identify a management focus to implement the plan?

2 How to make the plan a relevant and living document for everyone in the organisation?

3 How to monitor, measure and ensure that the assumptions behind the plan are still relevant?

4 How to manage changes involved in the plan?

5 What is meant by strategic management?

HOW TO IDENTIFY A MANAGEMENT FOCUS TO IMPLEMENT THE PLAN?

Often the hardest part of managing is for the manager to know where to exert limited time, energy and effort.

O O O O O O O O O

Case Study
DEVELOPING CRITICAL SUCCESS FACTORS

The Halfway project provides practical help and supported accommodation to people with learning difficulties. It employs 38 staff and operates in four local authority areas.

After reconsidering its mission, agreeing a strategic direction and priorities it set about identifying the key elements that it would need to work on to get from its current position to the intended one set out in the business plan.

After identifying specific aims for the organisation (eg. to develop a new service in a particular location) it also agreed eight factors that managers would need to work on to manage the successful competion of their aims and objectives. It would have been possible to have a much longer list. However, the team felt that it was better to focus all their effort on the eight points rather than to try to cope with more.

The factors were:

1 Much better communication between the main office and projects. Must feel that we are all part of one organisation. More attention to teamwork.

2 Need to reduce paperwork and duplication of systems. Enhanced use of new technology.

3 Better financial management system. We need to know exactly what each activity or project costs and have better control of costs in order to properly negotiate contracts.

4 More attention to securing the long term commitment of our current individual and corporate donors. Persuading existing donors to give regularly and feel a strong loyalty link with us.

5 Our name, image and identity needs reviewing. Need for crisper, more modern and better understood public image.

6 Need to develop our skills and expertise in marketing, negotiating and costing service agreements and contracts.

7 Must develop a commitment to innovation, experimentation and new work. Innovation must be encouraged and rewarded.

8 Need for the two senior managers to spend more time on the strategic development of the organisation and less on detailed "micro" managing.

One established technique is to identify those factors that managers need to focus on if they are to be successful. These factors are known as critical success factors. They are the keys to the successful implementation and completion of the business plan. They are the things that the organisation believes it has to get right if it is to meet the plan.

Success factors are usually a mixture of "hard" elements (things that are tangible and easy to measure such as outputs) and "softer" issues (such as processes, working culture and styles of work).

It is important to limit the number of factors. Too many will lead to a lack of management focus. Once agreed, managers should work out exactly what they need to do to work on each issue and draw up clear and measurable action plans for each factor.

One management team attempted to draw up a list of critical success factors for their work. The final statement came from a session in which managers listed the things that they needed to change about how they managed, the things that they needed to improve and, importantly, the things that they needed to keep doing well. The final list was arrived at after some considerable negotiation within the management team. Responsibility for leading particular items were allocated to team members and review dates set. The critical success factors became the agenda for the management team for the coming year.

HOW TO MAKE THE PLAN A RELEVANT AND LIVING DOCUMENT FOR EVERYONE IN THE ORGANISATION?

Experience in several organisations suggests that the sooner people affected by a plan are involved in contributing to it the more likely it is that they will feel committed to its implementation. Even if early involvement has been achieved, there is a still a need to market and explain the plan internally to staff (existing and new staff), volunteers and supporters. Some national charities have developed an internal communication procedure to explain their mission and direction to staff as often people working within a part of the organisation fail to see the bigger picture of their work.

The following four examples show how some organisations have tried to explain and relate their business plan to individual employees.

◆ One national charity ensured that each member of staff received a copy of the business plan and had a meeting with their line manager. The meeting identified possible implications of the plan for their work, drew up an action plan for them and discussed future priorities.

◆ A housing association used the direction set out in its business plan as an input into a training needs analysis. The business plan identified a strategy that involved negotiating private finance for projects and operating in a competitive market. Consequently, the training needs analysis identified negotiating and marketing skills as important skill gaps within the organisation.

◆ One agency included in its staff appraisal scheme what contribution managers had made to meeting the business plan. It identified potential problems and helped managers focus their efforts.

◆ One charity produced a special staff newsletter explaining the business plan in detail. This was followed up by visits to every unit by a senior manager to discuss the plan in detail.

HOW TO MONITOR, MEASURE AND ENSURE THAT THE ASSUMPTIONS BEHIND THE PLAN ARE STILL RELEVANT?

Possibly the best test of the strategic aims and objectives is "can they be easily measured and monitored"? Often when something is hard to measure, it reveals that the objective for it is not clear.

The measures for the strategic aims should be mainly impact and outcome measures. They should focus on what was achieved, what needs were met and what longer term benefits were identified. The objective measures are likely to be progress, output/volume or reaction measures.

MONITORING THE PARTS OF THE PLAN

Business plans needs milestones. A number of measures should be established to check progress, identify problems early and enable action. The chart below sets out some of the things that could be monitored and suggests a possible time scale. The time scale would need to be fixed to take into account the particular circumstances of the organisation. For example an organisation managing several high risk projects to a tight budget might require more frequent reports.

Several different types of measures are available:

Progress measures	Reporting on specific work to date.
Volume or output measures	Reporting on the number using a service, occupancy rate or number of activities completed.
Reaction measures	Feedback from users.
Impact measures	Reports on the immediate benefits of the output.
Outcome measures	Longer term benefits and results.

ISSUE	MONITOR
Mission	Very occasionally, every 2 to 3 years.
Are the assumptions in the plan still valid?	Every six months or when deemed necessary.
Are the strategic aims still the right ones?	At least annually.
Progress/outcome each aim	Written report, produced quarterly or every six months.
Progress report on each objective	Monthly or quarterly written report.
Performance of management (critical success factors)	Quarterly team meeting.
Financial performance	Cost centre and income performance produced monthly. Cash flow review and forecast produced quarterly. Audit and balance sheet produced at least annually. Income future forecast produced every six months.

HOW TO MANAGE CHANGES INVOLVED IN THE PLAN?

Mikhail Gorbachev looking back at the experience of perestrokia talks about how key people did not change at all, instead they superficially adapted to it. They never fully accepted or committed themselves to the real changes involved in the project, they added some new words to their vocabulary, pretended to absorb it, but their practice and their behaviour remained the same.

An interesting way of looking at what changes are called for is the idea of first and second order change. First order change is change that takes place within the structure and culture as it currently exists. Second order changes require a profound change in how the organisation works if they are to take place at all. This is often called *"cultural change"*.

Second order change often involves risk, considerable effort and sometimes anxiety and conflict. In looking at the implications of the business plan, the following points could be considered:

EXAMPLES OF FIRST & SECOND ORDER CHANGE

FIRST ORDER CHANGE	SECOND ORDER CHANGE
Publishing a statement committing the organisation to "user participation".	Stopping doing something that has always been done because users no longer want it.
Proclaiming that the organisation is committed to equal opportunities and putting on equality training sessions for staff.	Taking a risk with with a new service to see if it is more relevant to a particular minority group.
Having a policy statement on good environmental practices.	Changing car mileage policies so to encourage better use of environmental resources.
Writing a quality assurance manual that sets out minimum service standards.	Not taking on a low fee contract, because you might not be able to keep to your quality standard.

◆ What "second order" change is involved in the plan?

◆ What will be the the risk involved in this change?

◆ How can we best manage this change?

◆ How will we know that the change has been achieved?

Strategic management is often particularly difficult in voluntary organisations. A problem frequently encountered as a result of a business planning exercise is what to do with activities that no longer fit the mission and aims of the plan. Being ruthless is often not tolerated or particularly effective in the

○ ○ ○ ○ ○ ○ ○ ○ ○

INNOVATION IN NOT FOR PROFIT ORGANISATIONS

"...public service institutions find it far more difficult to innovate than even the most "bureaucratic" company. The "existing" seems to be even more of an obstacle.

To be sure, every service institution likes to get bigger. In the absence of a profit test, size is the one criterion of success for a service institution and growth a goal in itself.

And then, of course, there is always so much more that needs to be done. But, stopping what has "always been done" and doing something new are equally anathema to service institutions, or at least excruciatingly painful to them."

Peter Drucker. 1984.   *reprinted with permission*

WHAT IF THINGS DO NOT FIT INTO THE STRATEGY?

Several organisations have experienced difficulties in deciding what to do with activities and functions that are established parts of the organisation, but, no longer fit with the direction agreed. Three examples of this include:

1 A national childrens' charity committed to non institutional care, but, still owns two large residential schools.

2 A voluntary organisation had a volunteer fund raising committee that raised annually decreasing amounts of money. The level of servicing and support it expected from the organisation made it hardly cost effective. The group was very reluctant to consider new ideas.

3 A charity that decided to move into advocacy, campaigning and rights work. It still had a core of users who turned up most days expecting a social and recreational day centre.

Several strategies exist in this situation:

◆ Do nothing and hope that it will come to a natural end.

◆ Put the activity on a minimum "care and contact" relationship in which time and money spent on it is tightly controlled.

◆ Plan an "exit strategy", where over time the activity is phased out and resources redeployed.

◆ Merge it into another organisation or encourage it to "float off" independently.

◆ Redirect it into another purpose more in line with the direction. If it is unable to make the change, after time, close it.

One manager observed that she spent more time dealing with the activities that did not fit the strategy than the ones that did. The following five points are useful in developing an "exit strategy":

1 Keep the end date firmly in mind. Draw up a "critical path" so that the end date is a central focus.

2 Keep people who work on, use and support the project well informed. Avoid surprises.

3 Organise a gradual programme of briefings, consultations, training, and support.

4 Look after the people involved. Acknowledge possible feelings of loss. Identify individual and group successes.

5 Try to end it on a high point.

longer term. Keeping running activities that are out of step with the rest of the organisation could eventually diminish the organisation's effort and leave it fragmented and drifting.

WHAT IS MEANT BY STRATEGIC MANAGEMENT?

A survey of headteachers published in 1992 examined what headteachers did with their time. A sample group of headteachers were asked to list what they considered to be the most important aspects of their role. Their list focused on "strategic" issues, curriculum development, managing change, forward planning and school development. Detailed examination of what they actually did showed that the vast majority of their time at school was spent on fragmented tasks that no one else was available to do; repairing the photocopier, making a sign or filling in for a sick colleague. It was as if all the strategic issues were continually pushed into taking a poor second or third place.

Different definitions of strategic management abound in management text books. The chart below sets out some of the differences between operational management (running the day to day work) and strategic management.

	OPERATIONAL MANAGEMENT	STRATEGIC MANAGEMENT
Focus	Day to day survival.	Long term development of organisation.
Objective	Keeping things going.	Finding better ways of doing things or exploring new ideas.
Change	Coping with imposed change.	Managing change and transition.
Motive	Creating stability.	Creating future possibilities.
Purpose	Keeping current services functioning.	Exploring new services and ensuring future role.
Process	Use of procedures and systems.	Focus on evaluation, direction and vision.
Decision making	By precedent or rule book.	Considering future choices and options.

It is not about being either an operational manager or a strategic manager. Someone who was entirely operational in their management role would probably suffer from not seeing the "big picture" and concentrate entirely on detail rather than the purpose. Equally, managers who focus entirely on strategic issues often lose touch with the realities of the organisation and are often dismissed as being aloof and impractical.

Strategic management in a voluntary organisation often involves the following six activities:

❶ Making sure that everyone in and around the organisation understands the organisation's purpose and values.

❷ Ensuring that the activities and projects connect together, that evaluation takes place, and that progress towards the mission and aims is measured.

❸ That the organisation keeps in touch with developments in the outside world. New needs, trends and opportunities are predicted and responded to.

❹ That the structures, systems and skills of the organisation fit the task. That the organisation is fit for its purpose.

❺ Managing change that will effect the organisation. Increasingly the changes are not linear ones (i.e. getting from A to B), but are about managing uncertainty, where change is likely, but, the details are not clear.

❻ Coordinating and organising forward planning through identifying strategies, contingencies and business planning.

THE IMPLICATIONS OF THE PLAN

Divide likely changes involved as a result of the plan into "first order" and "second order" changes. First order changes are changes that can be absorbed or managed within the current organisation's structures and culture. Second order changes are those that are likely to require change in the way that you work. List the kind of changes that might be involved, under the seven headings used by the McKinsey's 7-S framework

	first order change	second order change
Strategy (direction and priorities)		
Structure (organisational design)		
Staff (employment practices)		
Skills (competence and skill gaps)		
Systems (financial and management controls)		
Style (relations to users and image)		
Shared values (what is important about how we work)		

MAKING THE PLAN WORK

This exercise aims to help you to identify the factors that the people responsible for managing the plan will have to develop. As you work through the exercises note down any factor, process or attribute that you feel will be needed to successfully implement the plan.

❶ HIGH & LOW POINTS. All organisations have high points and low points. Draw a line of the organisation's history (or at least for as long as you have known it).

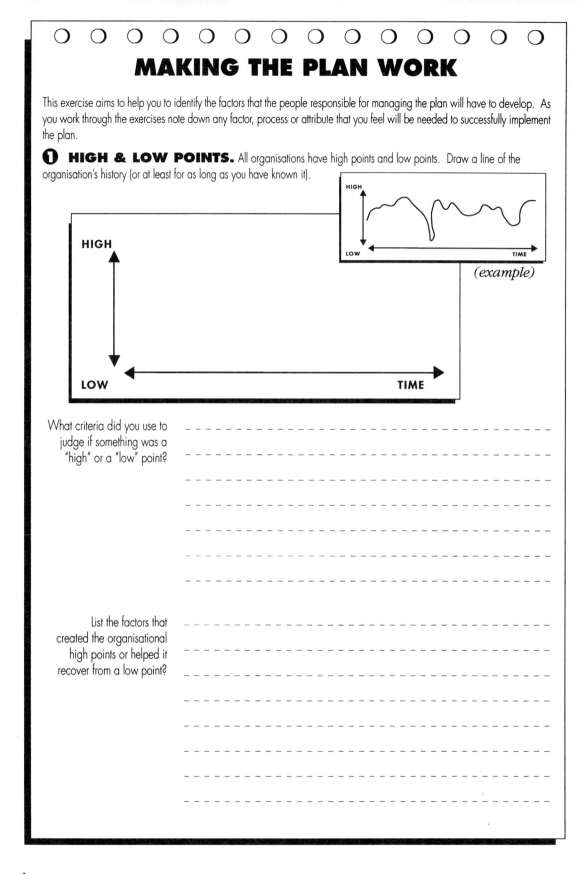

(example)

HIGH

LOW   **TIME**

What criteria did you use to judge if something was a "high" or a "low" point?

_ _

_ _

_ _

_ _

_ _

_ _

List the factors that created the organisational high points or helped it recover from a low point?

_ _

_ _

_ _

_ _

_ _

MAKING THE PLAN WORK

➋ SUCCESS FACTORS

Think of successful organisations that you know well. What are the factors that contribute to their success? Focus on internal factors & external factors.

Are any of these factors available to you in implementing your plan?

➌ KEY PROCESSES

Organisations are usually described in structural terms (departments, units etc.). Often the key to success is getting the key processes right. Processes usually cut across an organisation's structure and depend upon cooperation, team work and communication.

In terms of your plan what processes does the organisation need to get right?

Review your list

Try to identify a limited number (no more than eight) *critical success factors* that your organisation needs to focus on to successfully implement the plan.

➊ _____

➋ _____

➌ _____

➍ _____

➎ _____

➏ _____

➐ _____

➑ _____

MONITORING THE PLAN

This exercise will help you to monitor the progress of the plan and evaluate its longer term effectiveness.

What are the key milestones that can be used to monitor the plan's progress?

- -

- -

- -

- -

- -

How and when will the following elements of the plan be reviewed and monitored?

❶ MISSION	How will it be monitored and reviewed?	Frequency
Are the assumptions in the plan still valid?		
Are the strategic aims still the right ones?		
Progress/outcome of each aim		
Progress report on each objective		
Performance of management (critical success factors)		

MONITORING THE PLAN

② FINANCIAL PERFORMANCE

	How will it be monitored and reviewed?	Frequency
Performance to plan of each project/cost centre		
Overall financial performance		

In terms of outcomes and results how will you judge the plan's overall success?

_____
_____
_____
_____
_____
_____
_____
_____
_____
_____
_____
_____
_____
_____

103

SCENARIO PLANNING

Several organisations, notably the military and the oil industry have used imaginary scenarios as both a learning and planning tool. A possible future situation is described and participants work out how the organisation could respond to it and then evaluate the likely impact of their actions.

A housing organisation developed its annual staff residential around three scenarios:

❶ The decision by a major funder to withdraw its financial commitment by phasing it out over two years.

❷ A change in the political control and the managerial style within a local authority. The new leadership would be interested in partnerships and transferring the management of several projects from the public to the independent sectors.

❸ A decline in demand. A combination of reasons have led to a sharp fall in the numbers of referrals to a usually busy project. Financial, marketing and service plans would need to be quickly implemented.

Staff worked in teams to suggest short term and long term action plans, explore options, spot dangers and test out the organisation's current processes.

Extensive discussion followed on how the scenarios could have been anticipated or avoided, the importance of a coordinated response throughout the organisation and the need for contingency plans.

The outcome of the day was that all staff had some experience of strategic thinking, and several outline contingency plans have been produced (for example blueprints for possible projects should the opportunity arise).

Three months after the exercise, a similar situation to one of the scenarios did arise which tested the effectiveness of the plans and the process!

What scenarios could you design for your organisation?

_____

_____

_____

_____

_____

_____

_____

_____

_____

_____

What would be your organisation's likely response?

☐ Chaotic?   ☐ Strategic?   ☐ Coordinated?

☐ Planned?   ☐ Delayed?   ☐ Bureaucratic?

"SOFT" STRATEGY MISSING

A theatre had invested considerable time and money in producing a business plan. External consultants, residential weekends and considerable extra work by the finance officer had produced a final document. The plan looked impressive with detailed objectives, cash flow projections and measurable business targets.

Three months after the plan's production the theatre's director announced her intention to resign and live abroad. The announcement did not surprise anyone as for the past year she had often talked about her plans. The director had set the theatre up and in many respects it was an extentsion of her personality. Much of the theatre's "know how" was carried in her head. She had a considerable personal network of funders, contacts and supporters. Trustees and staff expressed fear and panic about the difficulty of replacing her and how much would be lost when she left.

The organisation had spent nearly a whole year planning. All the hard elements (costing, marketing plans, staffing levels etc) had been properly dealt with, but, one of the few things that could have been anticipated had been ignored.

Examples of soft strategy could include people, styles of work, goodwill, cooperation and partnerships?

What elements of soft strategy need to be thought about in your planning process?

READING LIST

Strategic management issues

The Strategic Management Blueprint.
Dobson & Starkey. Blackwell Business Books.

Strategic Management.
Bowman & Asch. Macmillan.

Innovation and Entrepreneurship.
Drucker. William Heinemann.

Learning To Lead.
Garratt.   Harper Collins.

Business Planning

Planning For The Future.
Martin & Smith. NCVO.

The Business Plan Workbook.
Barrow, Barrow & Brown.   Kogan Page.

Financial Issues

Making The Most of Your Business.
National Westminster Bank.

Costing For Contracts.
Callaghan. NCVO/Directory of Social Change.

Related issues

Managing The Non Profit Organisation.
Drucker. Harper Collins.

Outcome Funding.
Williams & Webb. NCVO.

Quality Of Service.
Lawrie. NCVO/Directory of Social Change.

SOFTWARE

Most spreadsheets will
make the financial planning elements
easier. Two American companies
have designed software for business
planning or strategic management.

Palo Alto's Business Plan Toolkit is very
strong on the financial planning
aspects and comes with a helpful
manual, although it would need some
minor adaption to United Kingdom
accounting procedures.

Idea Fisher Systems,
"Idea Fisher" programme
is a creative thinking tool and contains
useful interactive questions on strategic
thinking and vision. It also has a
separate add on module for strategic
planning work.

They are available from
most large software houses.